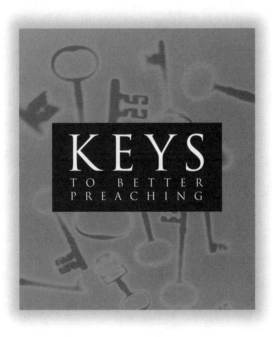

# KEYS
## TO BETTER
## PREACHING

# KEYS
## TO BETTER
## PREACHING

# JOHN
# GARLOCK

# KEYS TO BETTER PREACHING
## BY JOHN GARLOCK

*...How shall they believe*
*in Him of whom*
*they have not heard?*
*And how shall*
*they hear without*
*a preacher?*

ROMANS 10:14 (NKJV)

Unless otherwise indicated, all Scripture quotations are taken from the *King James Version* of the Bible.

First Printing 1992
Second Edition 2000
Third Printing 2003
ISBN 0-89276-961-0

In the U.S. write:
Kenneth Hagin Ministries
P.O. Box 50126
Tulsa, OK 74150-0126
1-888-28-FAITH
www.rhema.org

In Canada write:
Kenneth Hagin Ministries
P.O. Box 335, Station D
Etobicoke (Toronto), Ontario
Canada, M9A 4X3

**Introduction**

**Foreword**

If God has called you to preach, whether full-time or otherwise, you naturally want to do your best in fulfilling His call. Regardless of your degree of past experience — or inexperience — this manual can help you learn how to preach better. It provides a wealth of information from discoveries I've made during my many years of preaching — as well as information gleaned from shared experiences with many fellow ministers of the Gospel.

I am fully aware that there are thousands of books available on the subject of preaching, and that more appear every year. Each one has its strengths — but most share one of two serious weaknesses. Some are too theoretical. Others promulgate some single formula for sermon preparation as if it were the only way to do it. And few, if any, give adequate attention to the nitty-gritty details

of what to do with your voice, eyes, and body during sermon delivery. So I have earnestly sought to fill in the blanks of this very crucial knowledge in the pages of this text.

Combining my own pulpit experience with the various texts I have used in my teaching of Public Speaking and Homiletics for fifty years, I am confident that the principles laid out in the following chapters, if applied, will noticeably improve your preaching skills.

A very important part of the work of the five-fold ministry of prophet, apostle, pastor, evangelist, and teacher, is to preach or teach the truth of the Bible orally. Of course, any minister must also be willing to spend time praying for individuals and offering them counsel when they ask for it. But it is through teaching and preaching to an entire congregation that the minister of God's truth can usually exert the greatest amount of influence upon the greatest number of people.

Since the time of Christ, people have been spiritually born again into the Kingdom of God as they have responded to effective preaching. Though many decisions are made in private, it is probable that a majority of believers take the step of accepting Jesus as Savior because of a powerful public presentation of the Gospel. It is therefore very important that any evangelistic minister should know how to make such a presentation in the strongest possible way.

But evangelism is not the only reason a minister should know how to speak effectively. The spiritual health of believers after

they have accepted Christ depends very much upon the quality of the teaching and preaching they hear. If the minister does this part of his work well, his people will become more godly. They will also become equipped themselves to effectively share the Word of God as fellow ambassadors and soulwinners in Christ.

The material that follows is intended to help ministers improve their ability to teach and preach. Its presentation, however, is in no way meant to imply that technique alone is sufficient for a person to be a successful minister. Without the presence and anointing of the Holy Spirit, our efforts are in vain. But it is well-known that the Holy Spirit uses whatever tools we offer Him and that well-sharpened tools give Him better opportunities to use us.

There is no such thing as *one* universal and perfect way to preach. There is much room for variation in style and method. So you will not find in this manual any attempt to promote one particular formula as the answer to every problem. However, there are certain principles used by Jesus Himself and other skillful ministers, which can be consciously applied by any minister in the preparation and delivery of his/her message. These principles are simple and practical, and obey certain scientific laws of communication which have been proven throughout the centuries. May the information in these pages give you new power and impetus as you preach the Word!

**John Garlock**
**Bulverde, Texas**
**February 2000**

**A** prominent Texas defense lawyer with an acerbic tongue once greeted an evangelist friend of mine at the start of his eight-day evangelistic crusade with this remark: "I hope you're not one of those long-winded preachers. As an experienced communicator, I can tell you that no souls are saved after twenty minutes. The mind cannot absorb more than the seat can endure."

The evangelist responded: "I'm surprised at your contradictory behavior. As an attorney, when you address the jury and your twenty minutes are up, do you say 'Your Honor, ladies and gentlemen of the jury…my time is up…I rest my case.' No, you don't. You plead for the temporal welfare of your client, just as I plead for the eternal welfare of my audience. And if that takes more than twenty minutes, so be it." Understanding that explanation, the lawyer saw the idiocy of his position regarding the length of a sermon.

In his book, *Positive Preaching and the Modern Mind*, P. T. Forsyth says, "Brevity may be the soul of wit but the preacher is not a wit…. A Christianity of short sermons is a Christianity of short fibre."

Another peerless pulpiteer of yesteryear, Dr. Robert G. Lee, said, "Sermonettes by preacherettes produce christianettes."

Therefore, the art of preaching is not in the length of the sermon but in the ability to bridge the gap between the speaker and his audience with a Spirit-inspired message.

It has been wisely said that every sermon should seem like twenty minutes even if it is actually longer. It is from this premise that my good friend John Garlock's practical, educational, and much-needed book on the art of preaching has been produced. John Garlock is one of the great preachers and teachers of today. He was my mentor at the Bible school my wife and I attended many years ago, and we are grateful for his teaching. It is particularly gratifying for me to have John on the board of International Christian Mission (ICM), Inc. as a traveling professor to our Bible schools in different parts of the globe.

*Keys to Better Preaching* has been written as a practical resource and seeks to encourage and challenge all preachers to make known God's way of salvation in a manner that maximizes the message and minimizes the messenger. I believe this book will take its place as one of the best treatments available on the subject of preaching. It is my hope that this book will fall into the hands of all who have a heart to bring closure to the Great Commission by doing their part in sounding forth the Word of Life.

**Hin Hiong Khoo**
**Founder/President**
**International Christian Mission, Inc.**

# CHAPTER ONE

# WHAT IS PREACHING ALL ABOUT?

## THE LIVING, WRITTEN, AND SPOKEN WORD OF GOD

**P**reaching at its best is a manifestation of the *Living* Word, developed from the *written* Word, and delivered by the *spoken* Word.

The *Living* Word is Jesus Christ, and any preaching that doesn't reveal and glorify Him is not worthy of the name. Of course, many sermons lift up Christ in an indirect way, especially if they are based upon the Old Testament, but Jesus can be seen in the pages of Scripture from Genesis to Revelation. It

is therefore not too strong a statement to say that all sermons should help the listener grow in his comprehension and appreciation of Christ and His Good News.

The *written* Word is the Bible, and any preaching that is not based solidly upon *it* is something else and is not true Christian preaching. Contemporary testimony has its place also, as does reference to current news events and their bearing upon the Christian life. But these should not serve as the primary examples or illustrations when preaching the Bible's truth. The foundation of any Christian sermon must be some portion or portions of the Holy Scripture.

The *spoken* Word is the preacher's own oral proclamation of the living and written Word. A printed version is secondary, so in the purest sense, a sermon cannot be put in a book, though there is a glut of books consisting merely of recorded sermons. A sermon is defined as a "religious discourse delivered as part of a church service." Therefore, the live, audible presentation is a sermon's essence.

Included within the delivery of a sermon is the verbal exposition of the Bible's revelation projected through the dynamic use of the preacher's voice, the preacher's eye contact with the listeners, and the constant small adjustments made by the preacher as the audience responds to him. This is what the sermon is all about. A sermon is alive!

This manual is aimed at helping sincere preachers to better accomplish this important mission. Those who invest the time in studying and applying its principles will allow the *Living* Word to become more real, the *written* Word to become more clear, and the *spoken* Word to become more powerful.

## A Bible Formula for Preaching

Nehemiah 8:8 demonstrates the profound simplicity of the preacher's basic task.

*So they read in the book in the law of God distinctly, and gave the sense, and caused them to understand the reading.*

— Nehemiah 8:8

At a time when the people of Israel had long been out of touch with the Torah of Moses, the leadership undertook the task of reviving God's Law in Israel to make it the focus of their attention again. Notice the three important things done by Ezra's assistants:

1. *They read distinctly from the book.* This indicates attention to clear oral delivery. **The principles of good public speaking are important.**

2. *They gave the sense.* This shows an attention to exegesis and exposition. **Sound Bible scholarship is important.**

3. *They caused them to understand the reading.* This demonstrates a follow-through to a state of assimilation and

self-application by the audience. **The practical implications of the truth are also important.**

These three concepts applied by Ezra and his assistants remain valid for preaching in all times, places, and cultures.

The preacher's fundamental task is one of translation. He takes the words of Scripture and renders them alive and full of meaning to those who listen. The preacher is a transmission line and lens to make clearer what the Bible says. His work is to "start at the Book and end at the people."

Indeed, the three fundamentals of Nehemiah 8:8 have long been the foundation of classical Bible preaching and teaching. Many successful Bible schools have operated by simply gathering some eager students around a skilled teacher who takes them through a Bible passage verse-by-verse, stopping to explain and expound as he goes along. The essential elements are all there:

1. Read aloud a significant passage of the Bible.

2. Give a commentary on its meaning as your study has helped you understand it and as God has revealed it to you.

3. Explain and illustrate how the scriptural truths apply to the lives of your listeners.

With the right teacher and, of course, the right students, this elementary method has helped produce some excellent

> The preacher's fundamental task is one of translation. He takes the words of Scripture and renders them alive and full of meaning to those who listen. The preacher is a transmission line and lens to make clearer what the Bible says. His work is to "start at the Book and end at the people."

ministries. So be encouraged — it can still happen today! Preaching and teaching are not so complicated after all!

But we must never forget that the preaching ministry takes time to allow God's anointing to do His best work. I once asked a group of pastors in an underdeveloped country, "What is the difference between *teaching* and *preaching?*" I was startled by the answer. Most of them said, "The difference between teaching and preaching is that for teaching you must know something; for preaching, you just say, 'Blessed be the Lord,' and everything you say after that is automatically inspired." Although more sophisticated preachers would not put it so bluntly, some of them seem to believe the same falsehood: that preaching does not really need serious preparation.

The danger in Nehemiah's three-fold preaching approach is lack of prayer and preparation. If a preacher hasn't spent the time necessary to understand the sermon himself, he may depend too much upon the impromptu thoughts of the moment. He may say whatever comes to mind about the passage and skip over the parts he finds difficult, leaving the hearer with his own shallow understanding of the Bible rather than a solid, balanced grasp.

The "Nehemiah method" is obviously subject to a wide range of quality — from the truly profound to the cheap and inadequate. But for the beginning preacher who is still groping for organizational skills, the method offers a simple way to get started, and can be a very satisfactory approach to preaching in its most fundamental (though bare-bones) form.

## What Is Homiletics?

*Homiletics* is "the science and art of the preparation and delivery of sermons." (Do not confuse this academic term, however, with the art and science of biblical interpretation, which is referred to as *Hermeneutics*.)

The definition of homiletics employs four important terms:

Science

Art

Preparation

Delivery

## Scientific Preaching?

As a *science*, preaching is governed by the laws of nature, especially those pertaining to human nature and communication, not just those of the spirit. It also touches phonetics, acoustics, semantics, psychology, and many other disciplines. So the fact that preaching deals with sacred truth does not exempt it from the rules of good communication.

Marvelously inspired material may fail to reach its target if the preacher ignores the principles of homiletics, which are applicable to any form of public address.

## Preaching an Art?

Even though preaching does involve some scientific qualities (qualities which can be reproduced to produce the same effect), preaching is much more than a science. As an *art*, preaching has room for an infinite variety of styles and creative innovations, just as do other arts. There is no one "right" way to preach, and each preacher has the privilege of developing his own presentation style. One preacher can rarely copy the style of another with sure success.

There are many ways to drive an automobile: fast or slow, carefully or recklessly, aggressively or timidly, expertly or clumsily. Yet to successfully arrive at their desired destinations, all drivers must conform to the limitations of the car, road, and traffic. Otherwise, they will face sure disaster. The same is true of preaching. The *science* of preaching provides a knowledge of the basic "rules" within which the preacher must operate. But it is the *art* of preaching that gives scope to his own peculiar inspiration and unique creativity.

Indeed, most of the "rules" of good preaching, including those this manual will emphasize, may sometimes be violated by some very successful preachers. Do not be tempted to use those exceptions as excuses to ignore the rules. It is a simple fact that exceptions are occasionally appropriate for special reasons and in special circumstances. As Beethoven and Bach sometimes, for creative purposes, did not follow the accepted principles of melody and harmony, so a skilled preacher will sometimes, for special effect, do something not usually advisable. But for most preachers, most of the time, the principles we set forth in this manual are the way to get the best results.

## Preaching Is Announcing

Fundamental to both the history and the etymology of preaching is the idea of *proclamation*. The preacher is an announcer of the truth. He is a town crier of the news of salvation and the grace of God. Although he should be persuasive, his task is not so much to argue as to declare. He is like the fortunate one in a party of thirsty desert travelers who turns to tell the others that he has found water. He is like one of the lepers at the siege of Samaria (*see* 2 Kings 7:9) who feels a duty to share the booty.

God miraculously healed a blind man in China many years ago as a missionary prayed for him. The man became a fervent believer in Christ but, to the missionary's disappointment, soon disappeared from the church. Many days later, the missionary looked up to see the former blind man walk into the mission compound holding the end of a rope that trailed behind him. Holding on to the rope behind him was a whole procession of other blind men he had rounded up to receive the same help he had found. This is a good analogy of the work of a preacher: to share with others the wonder and joy of his discoveries in Christ.

In this sense, the emphasis of the preacher is different from that of the teacher. We will later enumerate a number of situational differences between the two ministries. For now it is sufficient to point out that the preacher is not just a researcher or a seeker after truth (though in his preparation he works as such), but he is one who knows what he knows and tells it with confidence to those who are uninformed or less certain of the truth. The unknown author of the following verse captures this preaching mission very well:

> He who knows not, and knows not that he knows not —
> he is a fool; shun him!
> He who knows not, and knows that he knows not —
> he is simple; teach him!
> He who knows, but knows not that he knows —
> he is asleep; wake him!
> He who knows, and knows that he knows —
> he is wise; follow him!

The preacher who preaches things he believes only in a lukewarm or equivocal way courts calamity. Preaching may therefore be thought of as *the sharing of strong convictions*. The preacher must speak with a sure word and a positive spirit.

## Preaching and Prophecy

Preaching is also, in a very literal sense, *speaking for God*. In this meaning, it performs a *prophetic* function. In Scripture, the messages of the prophets were largely sermons of correction or encouragement. Their utterances were mingled with predictions, to be sure, but prediction is not the essential element in prophecy. *Prophecy* is simply speaking what God wants people to hear.

*Preaching,* when it consists of a message that is truly from God to the people, is essentially indistinguishable from prophecy, whether or not the preacher makes any claim to being a prophet. His *office* (or chief function in the Body of Christ) may not be that of a prophet, but in the larger sense, he is certainly ministering prophetically when he is preaching what he has been directed by God to preach.

All of this means that preaching is not only a privilege but a very serious and important business. Preaching the Word of God is not something to do because one has no other work or is seeking a livelihood. It is a calling to a noble and mediatorial task that partners with God in His great plan of communicating His truth to the world.

John 15:21-27 names every member of God's partnership who has been communicating His divine will since Jesus visited the earth.

> The Father is...*him that sent...* (v.21).
> The Son is the One who has...*come and spoken...*
> (v.22).
> The Holy Spirit is the One who...*shall testify...* (v.26).
> And the disciples are those who...*also shall bear*
> *witness...* (v.27).

These four partners make up God's Cosmic Communication Corporation, and you are part of the group!

## God's Communication Principles — Revelation, Mediation, Illumination

Now, as we complete this first chapter, we must mention the non-homiletic communication principles of God which must be powerfully evident during both sermon preparation and public presentation. These principles have to do with personal devotional time spent in preparation and should always be incorporated to ensure that your sermon is *ALIVE*.

First of all, though the use of every study help that will be presented in later chapters is a must for intelligent presentation, if the Holy Spirit is not resident in sermon preparation, the message may be true but incomplete. So the first principle of God's communication is divine *revelation*. It is through His divine revelation that God communicates with man and is willing to draw aside the curtain of His transcendence to give us knowledge and guidance far beyond what we could ever find for ourselves.

Next, the principle of *mediation* connotes the fact that God has chosen to use human instruments to convey His revelation, to bridge the communication gap that stands between Himself and man, and to express Himself to humanity through yielded humanity.

Finally, the principle of *illumination* allows the Word to become personal to the listener and can speak very specifically to him as the preacher (mediator) brings it to bear upon his real-life situation.

These three together — revelation, mediation, and illumination — comprise the process through which God has chosen to make known His grace and truth. It has pleased Him "by the foolishness of what is preached" (*see* 1 Corinthians 1:21) to save people over the centuries.

And when you preach, remember that Jesus Christ Himself has prayed for you and your listeners with these words:

*"For I have given to them the words which You have given Me; and they have received them, and have known surely that I came forth from You; and they have believed that You sent Me"*(John 17:8 *NKJV*).

*"I pray for them…"* (v.9).

*"As You sent Me into the world, I also have sent them into the world"* (v.18).

*"I do not pray for these alone, but also for those who will believe in Me through their word…"* (v.20).

# CHAPTER TWO

# PREACHING OR TEACHING — WHAT'S THE DIFFERENCE?

**S**ome people are distracted by trying to separate *teaching* from *preaching* as if each were entirely different from the other. There are some differences, but the differences are not "entire"…and there are very many similarities. To help clarify our thinking, here are some observations about each. Notice that the listed differences are mainly differences in the *situation* or the *emphasis*, not in the *style* or the *importance*.

———

# COMPARISONS BETWEEN TEACHING AND PREACHING

| PREACHING | TEACHING |
|---|---|
| One-time audience. | Same audience more than once. |
| Uses mostly lecture method. | Uses a variety of methods. |
| Often a larger audience. | Usually a smaller audience. |
| Presentation stands alone. | Presentation is part of a series. |
| Wide variety of listeners. | Listeners much alike. |
| Audience questions are rare. | Questions are invited. |
| Little note-taking. | Note-taking is expected. |
| Little or no testing. | Tests (exams) are likely. |
| Bible is the only textbook. | Other textbooks are likely. |
| Homework is very rare. | Homework is very common. |
| Session length is more flexible. | Session length is more rigid. |
| Emotional appeal is acceptable. | Emotional appeal less usual. |
| Structure is less visible. | Structure is emphasized. |

Remember, the preacher who preaches things he believes halfheartedly or equivocally courts calamity. And the same is true for teaching. The teacher's audience may be made up of more studious listeners, so his preparation and presentation techniques may call for extra biblical resources and audience

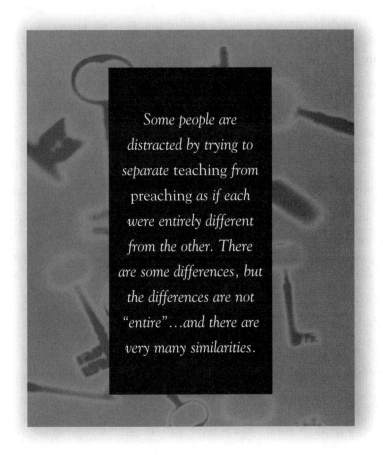

*Some people are distracted by trying to separate teaching from preaching as if each were entirely different from the other. There are some differences, but the differences are not "entire"...and there are very many similarities.*

interaction. Both preacher and teacher should spend sufficient time in preparing the message, and it should be presented in an orderly, memorable fashion. Preaching and teaching should convey truth and be anointed and inspiring.

Much effective preaching is done in a style that some people think more suitable for teaching, and vice-versa. There is no

solid wall between the two, and *the principles of communication we are dealing with are equally applicable to both*. We will frequently refer to both in this manual, although "preaching" will be the term we use most often. With few exceptions, the preaching principles examined in this study will apply equally to both methods of delivery.

If you are serious about preaching, you must also be willing to teach. In fact, most aspiring preachers entering the ministry will often have opportunities to teach sooner and much more frequently than preaching opportunities.

For example, you may already have some experience in teaching a Sunday school class. If not, you may soon have such an opportunity. So do not scorn such opportunity, no matter the age group. Teaching God's Word is excellent practice for preaching, as well as an opportunity to help those you teach to grow in His knowledge and will.

Teachers who teach well can be preachers who preach well. If you can do one well, you will be able to do the other at least passably.

In chapter 3 we'll look at the differences that separate preaching and speech-making.

# CHAPTER THREE

# THE PREACHER — A SPEECH-MAKER?

**R**ecognized as a spiritual and divinely guided activity, preaching is much more than just a specialized form of public speaking. Yet the rules of good public speaking apply to preaching just as they do to all forms of public address. An automobile driver is not exempt from the rules of the road nor the laws of physics just because he may be on a spiritual errand such as taking someone to Sunday school. Neither is a painter free to ignore the principles of line, form, and color just because he is creating a likeness of Christ instead of the portrait of a politician or a movie star. Likewise a preacher is not exempt from the limits that constrain common speech-making such as acoustics just because he is presenting spiritual truth.

One of the most serious mistakes a preacher can make is to assume that because his purposes are noble, he need not study the techniques which render a speaker effective. In fact, the importance of God's spoken message requires even more finely honed speaking skills in His public speakers than those of some-one dealing with less vital subject matter. A preacher should know everything any good public speaker knows . . . and more.

So, unspiritual as it may seem, in this chapter we will sum-marize some facts about public speaking, and see how they apply to Bible preaching.

## Kinds of Speaking

Secular speeches may employ a variety of styles, techniques, methods, purposes, and qualities to successfully strengthen each presentation. These may be classified in many ways, including the following:

### The Formal Speech

Any kind of spoken presentation can be classified by how much formality is used.

A *formal speech* is an oral presentation that has been com-pletely thought-out and written down before its delivery. This sort of formal presentation is not considered formal because it is read from a manuscript. It is considered formal because the words of its message have been determined beforehand. It is still considered formal even if it is memorized and no notes are used.

## The Extemporaneous Speech

An *extemporaneous speech* is an oral presentation in which ideas have been predetermined with no detailed wording. This is the kind of speech used in most sermons today. It is also the most popular speech in the world of politics and entertainment. Presidents, newscasters, and other public figures try to appear as if they're speaking spontaneously, even though they are working from an outline that has recorded phrases and key thoughts.

## The Impromptu Speech

An *impromptu speech* is a public address that has had no specific preparation before its delivery. This kind of speech can be excellent if the speaker has a rich background of experience on the speaking topic. *Impromptu* simply means "without preparation."

It is said that C. H. Spurgeon would sometimes call upon his homiletics students to give an impromptu sermon — which was a daunting experience for most. One exceptionally short student, when called upon, made his way to the front of the class and preached this "message":

"My sermon is about Zacchaeus...and contains three thoughts:

> First, Zacchaeus was a very small man; so am I!
>
> Second, Zacchaeus found himself up a tree; so do I!
>
> Third, Zacchaeus came down quickly; so will I!"

Thereupon the student ran back to his seat, and Spurgeon was heard to mutter, "Son, I think you'll make it."

## Speech Styles

Any speech occasion can also be classified as to the *style* it uses:

A *dramatic* speech emphasizes its message by the playing out of a role or roles for the benefit of the audience. This is powerful when done properly, but not many preachers use it. A few have successfully made a ministry of doing dramatic impersonations of the apostle Paul or other Bible characters. Such drama can be effective from behind or near the pulpit. However, a full dramatic presentation requires the use of costumes, scenery, and special lighting.

*Role-playing* is a certain kind of drama in which the action performed is mainly for the benefit of the participating "actors" rather than for an audience. Teachers have found this to be an effective teaching method because students can better understand

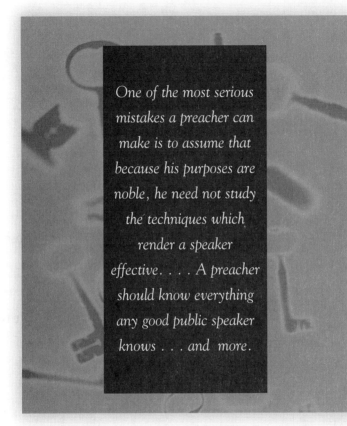

*One of the most serious mistakes a preacher can make is to assume that because his purposes are noble, he need not study the techniques which render a speaker effective. . . . A preacher should know everything any good public speaker knows . . . and more.*

the emotions of a Bible story when they try to take on those emotions themselves.

*Interpretive reading* presents formal material with emotional expression but without the use of costumes, special lights, or the scenery used in full drama. This form of speaking grazes the dramatic element but doesn't go all the way.

A preacher may profitably use this style when:

- Giving an illustration

- Re-enacting a dialogue

- Telling an exciting story, biblical or otherwise

- Reciting a poem

- Quoting a famous person

*Storytelling* involves the special techniques of narrative. Most often studied by those who work with children, presenting truth in story form is a public speaking skill that every communicator should master. Stories are not the only kind of illustrations a preacher can use, but they surely are one of the most effective. Jesus taught the unknown truths of God's spiritual kingdom through known truths on earth predominantly by using this engaging form of public speaking.

*Questions and answers.* Sometimes called the Socratic method because Socrates was so fond of it, this method of teaching leads listeners to reach the conclusion the speaker has in mind through inviting student's questions rather than making declarations. It is not a major technique of preaching.

*Audio-visual aids* should probably not be considered as a separate method of presentation, but as a help or reinforcement for many other methods. Although we think of it in connection with teaching, a sermon can often be presented in a more powerful way with the aid of posters, charts, or projected materials. Giving people something to look at as well as something to listen to is generally a good communication style.

*Discussion* provides a public speaking forum in which a whole group of people can examine a topic or search for consensus in response to a problem. A preacher is sometimes involved in discussion, but it is not a preaching style. However, the open-minded attitude that makes a discussion successful is also a very useful attitude in sermon *preparation*.

*Debate* is a speech forum that provides for the presentation of two distinct positions on an issue. Usually contradictory in their views, each debater takes the attitude that he alone is right and attempts to persuade listeners to agree. The typical debate situation is found in a court of law. Both opposing sides come with committed positions to defend, and attempt to persuade the jury to agree with their position. Debate, like discussion, is not a preaching style. However, the persuasion skills of a debater are very useful to a preacher in sermon *presentation*.

*Lecture* is the oldest and most traditional form of public speaking. Because this speaking form involves straight speaker-to-listener speech, it can convey more facts in less time than any other method, and is therefore the style most often used for preaching. It is also the style that can most easily cause boredom.

But lectures can be inspiring and engaging if the Holy Spirit is involved in the preparation and delivery process!

## What's the Purpose?

Another way speech can be classified is according to its purpose. Why is this speech being made? The answer is *always* one or more of the following:

> To be INTERESTING (motivating the hearer to listen).
>
> To be CLEAR (helping the listener to understand).
>
> To be CONVINCING (persuading the listener of something).
>
> To produce ACTION (inspiring the listener to respond.)

None of these are normally recognized preaching goals. But it is true that any sermon should accomplish these things, or it will not be effective.

Now let's move on to chapter 4 and take a closer look at the *aim* of effective preaching.

# CHAPTER FOUR

# WHAT MUST I AIM FOR?

The goals listed at the end of the previous chapter always constitute the aims of *all* speakers — including preachers. A detailed examination of these goals will help us understand how a good speaker accomplishes his desired results.

Remember, any public speaker's goals should be: to be *interesting*, to be *clear*, to be *convincing*, to *produce action*. Look at the order of this list. It progresses from the easiest goal to the

most difficult. And for a speaker to achieve one goal on the list, he must sequentially accomplish the ones before it. This means:

A speech may be *interesting* but accomplish nothing else.

To be *clear*, it must first be *interesting*.

To be *convincing*, it must be both *interesting* and *clear*.

To produce *action*, it must be *interesting*, *clear*, and *convincing*.

Each of these goals for listener engagement is accomplished by certain presentation techniques. The following list is not exhaustive, but it does provide some ideas that can help a speech (or a sermon) reach its goals.

**1.** To be interesting (motivating the audience to listen).

Secular examples would include *the work of comedians and other entertainers* and *"after dinner" speeches.*

Speaking topics that can be counted on for general and universal interest include:

*Whatever is novel or unusual — whether good or bad. Newness attracts attention.*

*Whatever is closely connected to the life of the listener. People care about "self."*

*Drama — with its accompanying emotions of love, hate, pride, jealousy, fear, greed, sympathy, etc.*

*Humor* — *though varying greatly from place to place and culture to culture.*

**2.** To be clear (helping the listener to understand).

Secular speaking examples in which clarity is a must include *orientation talks, explanations, announcements, instructions, and descriptions.* Religious examples include *doctrinal exposition of all kinds.*

Ways to enhance clarity include:

*Right vocabulary. Use not only a correct word but the* best word.

*Right order of presentation.*

*Skillfully presented examples and illustrations.*

*Diagrams and other visual aids.*

**3.** To be convincing (persuading the listener of something).

Speaking examples in which convincing the audience is the goal include *political talks, sales presentations, legal summaries in a courtroom, and evangelistic appeals.*

Convincing techniques which carry persuasive power include the following:

*Enthusiastic suggestion. People are swept along by enthusiasm, logical or not.*

*Repetition. A statement heard often enough will tend to be accepted.*

*Friendliness.* People tend to believe a friend, but doubt an enemy.

*Association.* People tend to accept an idea espoused by a person or organization they already respect.

Making a "straw man" of opposing views — *constructing a weak case for the opposition.*

Arousing fears of any alternative — *showing the likely results of opposing views.*

Logical argument — *showing that reason inevitably leads to the desired conclusion.*

Logic is mentioned last in this list because, contrary to much opinion, most of the other items are actually more effective in persuasion.

**4.** To produce action (inspiring the listener to respond by doing).

Speaking forums which seek to produce action include *sales presentations, fund-raising talks, speeches on political and social issues,* and *evangelistic invitations.*

Ways to produce listener action include:

*Suggesting some action in* accord *with what has been presented.*

*Offering a graduated path of small, easy, logical steps.*

*Providing a model to follow.*

*Giving reminders of the benefits of the action.*

These may not be the goals or the methods we usually recognize for preaching and teaching. In fact, some of them raise important ethical questions. A preacher should never be dishonest just to get results. He must never take the attitude that the end justifies the means.

On the other hand, a preacher cannot reject the facts of human psychology. People think in certain ways, and are led to conclusions according to some identifiable principles. Jesus employed excellent psychology when He said, *...he that is without sin among you, let him cast a stone...* (John 8:7). Paul had keen psychological insight when he shouted to a crowd that was half Pharisee and half Sadducee, *...I am a Pharisee, the son of a Pharisee...* (Acts 23:6).

Techniques of themselves are not necessarily moral or immoral — they are amoral. And they work — whether for good or bad. They could be used to promulgate lying propaganda or to bring people to repentance. The techniques don't care. They are simply realistic and effective principles of communication, and every preacher should know and understand them.

## Learn From the Master

Jesus' ministry was always interesting, clear, and convincing, and it produced action on the part of His audience. His communication with the woman at the well of Samaria (*see* John 4) is a valuable demonstration of good communication. In this instance, His audience was small (one person), but He did the important things a preacher or teacher should always do. It is possible to analyze His method in different ways. But in connection with the goals we have just been discussing, here are four steps which correlate well with those ideas:

1. *Capture the listener's attention*. This may be done in hundreds of ways. One frequently useful way is by surprise. Jesus surprised the woman at the well by asking for a drink — and immediately He captured her attention and aroused her curiosity.

2. *Connect with the listener's interests*. Every person has concerns that are uppermost in his or her mind. Jesus began His conversation with the woman at the well by bringing up the topic of *water*, which was her very reason for being there. And from then on He held her interest.

3. *Stimulate the listener's desire*. A preacher must not talk just about theories or doctrines. He must show concern for his listeners by talking about something that ministers to their needs. Jesus offered the woman who came to draw water the prospect of a perpetual supply of "living water."

4. *Invite the listener's action or participation*. A preacher should not simply state a truth and walk away. He should provide a suggested step for the listener to take in response to his message. Jesus asked the woman to bring her husband, and when the

> *Techniques of themselves are not necessarily moral or immoral — they are amoral. And they work — whether for good or bad. They could be used to promulgate lying propaganda or to bring people to repentance. The techniques don't care. They are simply realistic and effective principles of communication, and every preacher should know and understand them.*

disciples arrived at the well, she went into town and brought out everyone who would come.

## Put Yourself in the Place of the Listener

Another way to approach your task as a preacher is to start by analyzing the attitudes or qualities of the listener. Once we understand where the listener is mentally and emotionally, we can speak to him with a better chance of being heard and understood.

Some listeners may be eager, alert, receptive, intelligent, imaginative, and quick to grasp the truths you are presenting. *But it is not wise to assume that all listeners are so perceptive.* Always assume that your listeners share the following tendencies and preach accordingly.

## 1. Boredom

It is a serious mistake to assume that your listeners will sit on the edge of their pews in breathless anticipation of what you will say. It is much safer to assume that they arrived at church bored and indifferent to anything you may be wanting to say…and are highly suspicious that you are about to make their condition worse.

### Overcoming Boredom

The antidote to this boredom is to *start a fire* by saying or doing something that will stimulate the listener's immediate interest. Jesus "started a fire" at Jacob's well by asking the Samaritan woman for a drink. By her response, we know she did not expect Him to speak to her at all. His action was a surprise and piqued her interest.

## 2. Self-interest

Each listener has his own life along with its worries, aches, and pains. He has rent to pay and a variety of other responsibilities. And he also has his own personal dreams. So he is not automatically interested in what you have to say. You must show him — and quickly — that what you are saying has a direct relationship to his interests, desires, and well-being.

### Dealing with self-interest

The antidote for this human tendency toward self-interest is to *build a bridge* that will quickly connect your subject with the innate or latent interests of the listener. The Samaritan woman came to the well because she was interested in water, so Jesus began His conversation with the subject of water.

## 3. Lack of imagination

Never assume that your listeners catch on easily. This is a very important key to effective preaching. Listeners must be shown, not just told. They need you to spell your message out for them. They need pictures and plenty of examples.

### Overcoming lack of imagination

The antidote for a lack of listener imagination is to *open many windows*, which means to use numerous vivid illustrations that clarify meaning. During His time with the Samaritan woman, Jesus drew a word-picture of a continuous internal spring of water.

## 4. Weak Memory

When a preacher shoots out a series of truths to his listeners, it's like handing each of them twenty eggs, one after another.

It is very unlikely that the preacher's audience will get home safely with all those eggs because they have no way to keep them together.

## Overcoming weak memory

The antidote for weak memory is to *offer a basket* to your listeners, by presenting your material in a memorable outline or "structure." This is essentially a *list* of ideas. Your listeners will remember better if you present them with three reasons, two essentials, five steps, or seven weapons.

# 5. Uncertainty of Action

Even when a listener pays close attention to a reasonably well-presented message, he may not end up with a clear idea of what he should do in response to the message. The implications may escape him, and he may wonder, *Where do I go from here?*

## Dispelling uncertainty

The antidote for action uncertainty is to *plant a signpost* by pointing the listener to the appropriate response for the message you present. Be sensitive. If your admonition is too personal and specific, he may resent it. But it is important to give some clear indication of what he ought to do after having heard your sermon. You may call upon him for some action on the spot by inviting him to lift a hand for prayer or to take a step of commitment by coming forward. You may even want to suggest

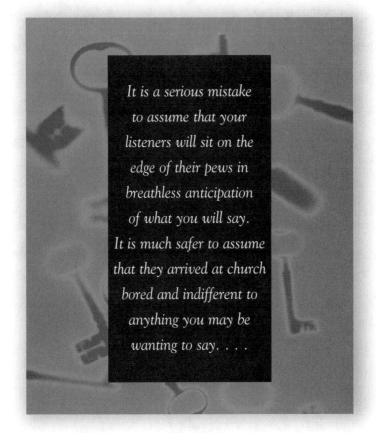

It is a serious mistake
to assume that your
listeners will sit on the
edge of their pews in
breathless anticipation
of what you will say.
It is much safer to assume
that they arrived at church
bored and indifferent to
anything you may be
wanting to say. . . .

some specific course of action for the week or month that lies ahead.

These five listener attitudes and their antidotes are not in themselves the "answer" to effective preaching. But they do provide some effective keys when considering your audience. Of course, to be effective, your sermon should be anointed and worthy of their full attention.

Self-interest *bridge building* and boredom-fighting *fire light-ing* should be the introduction aim of any sermon. Action-inspiring *signpost planting* should be the focus at the conclusion. Your aim in between should be to *open many imagination win-dows* while *offering a solid information basket* to allow your listeners to take home the sermon's impacting truths.

# CHAPTER FIVE

# WHAT GOES INTO A SERMON?

Every specialty has its own vocabulary, and preaching is no exception. To understand the history, functions, and the processes of preaching, we must give attention to some terms that define the materials and concepts the preacher works with. The following are the chief elements involved in a sermon.

## The Text

The text is the passage or portion of Scripture with which a sermon deals. Each sermon usually has *one* major text, with additional quoted passages to support it. By the end of a well-presented sermon, listeners should be able to recall and identify the important content of the text. The text should bring to mind the sermon, and the sermon should bring to mind the text.

Occasionally a preacher may use several different passages and give equal importance to each. In such a case, each of the passages is called a *complementary* (not complimentary) text.

Example:

Sermon Title: "Questions for Fugitives"

Text 1. Genesis 3:9: "Where are you?"

Text 2. Genesis 4:9: "Where is your brother?"

Text 3. 1 Kings 19:13: "What are you doing here?"

Example:

Sermon Title: "Facing the Future"

Text 1. Luke 12:17: "What shall I do?"

Text 2. Matthew 19:16: "What good thing shall I do?"

Text 3. Acts 16:30: "What must I do to be saved?"

A preacher should not form the habit of jumping through several scriptures to assemble his sermon, so the complementary text method should be used only occasionally. It is usually best for a sermon to concentrate upon a single text.

## Sermon Subject

The sermon's subject, of course, basically identifies what the message will be about. A memorable sermon must be about a definable *something*, not everything in general. One frequent mistake made by inexperienced preachers is attempting to cover more than one subject in the same sermon. Some speed all the way from Genesis to Revelation, but this is not good preaching. The sermon should have one clear subject and use a text and other attending scriptures that relate directly to that subject. If a listener is later asked what Sunday's sermon was about, he should be able to answer clearly and simply.

## The Title

The title is simply the "name" a preacher gives his sermon. The title may or may not include the actual name of the sermon subject. It may be deliberately mysterious in order to stimulate interest. For example, a sermon that deals with the subject of the love of God may be entitled "The Greatest Thing in the World." A well-thought-out title can light the interest fire and open an imagination window before the sermon begins. Just be careful not to use titles which make unrealistic promises or are misleading. Titles to avoid — for obvious reasons — include: "Who Is the Antichrist?" and "How Long Till Judgment Day?" Such titles should be used sparingly, if at all, because some people will hold you accountable to answer the question.

## The Proposition

A sermon is not ready to preach until its preacher can state its proposition clearly, if only to himself. The sermon proposition is a one-sentence summary that is sometimes called the sermon "thesis." It is not a description or even an extended title of the sermon — it is *the sermon* put into one sentence. It must be in a form that would make sense if spoken aloud to the congregation, although it is not necessarily used in this way. It is a means of disciplining a preacher's preparation by forcing him to boil down the essence of his thoughts until they can be summed up in one single sentence.

## The Outline

A sermon outline provides the structural framework for a sermon similar to a "trellis" on which roses grow. In this manual, I have chosen to refer to it most often as the *structure* because "outline" is so often evocative of complex rules, subpoints, and sub-subpoints. Such a complicated arrangement of any sermon is not only unnecessary, it is actually undesirable. The adding of too many points and sub-points can lead to the Genesis-to-Revelation kind of sermon mentioned earlier. Simply think of the *outline* as a "structured list" of the ideas that you want to get across. These ideas are the "points" of the outline.

You may of course have "sub-ideas" under each one, but these need not be assigned letters or numbers to share with the

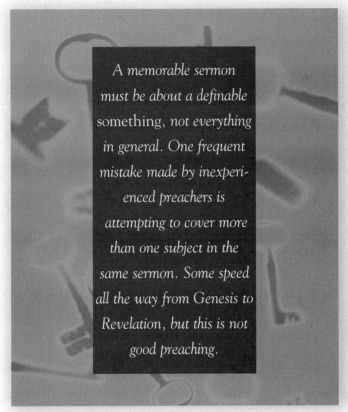

A memorable sermon must be about a definable something, not everything in general. One frequent mistake made by inexperienced preachers is attempting to cover more than one subject in the same sermon. Some speed all the way from Genesis to Revelation, but this is not good preaching.

audience. All a sermon normally needs as an outline is a sequence of the main thoughts.

Remember: Outline points are *ideas*, not scriptures or illustrations. The illustrations or scriptures associated with each sermon idea may be placed in parentheses *after* the statement of the idea (as reminders), but the *idea* is the outline point.

Outlined ideas may be expressed by single words, phrases, or complete sentences. Brevity is an important virtue here, as the main reason for structure is to aid the listener's memory.

Example:

### Title:

### What the Church Needs

### Text: Revelation 3:18

1. True Value ("...gold refined in the fire...")

2. True Virtue ("...white garments, that you may be clothed...")

3. True Vision ("...eye salve, that you may see...")

## Notes

Sermon notes consist of any written aids that assist the preacher's memory during the course of his presentation. The term, as we use it here, does not apply to subject materials that were researched or used during preparation. Most often the notes will contain the structure (outline) of the sermon, but these notes may also contain reminder facts such as statistics, names, quotations, etc. A preacher can learn to preach without using notes to remind him of the structure — but in order to do this with excellence, he must take the time to commit the entire structure to memory.

The best notes consist of brief reminder words that are arranged in vertical groups. Long horizontal sentences spread across a page are confusing and therefore don't make good notes. Think vertically!

The paper or card used for notes should be no larger than a page of the Bible you are using. This will help keep the audience's attention from focusing on these "reminders" unnecessarily. The more familiar you are with your message, the less you will need to refer to your notes — but you need never be ashamed of using notes. It is certainly better to have notes and not need them than to need them and not have them. Have your notes prepared, even if you think you will not use them.

## Illustrations

A sermon illustration is anything the preacher uses to create a picture in the mind of the listeners. The mental picture in turn causes them to understand and personalize the truth being presented. The following may all be considered illustrations:

- A story

- A comparison

- A description

- A figure of speech (idiomatic expression)

- A proverb

- A poem

- A prose quotation

- A diagram or chart

- A drawing

- A three-dimensional object

Mental images are the windows through which God's truth enters the mind and heart of the listener. So a preacher should have at least one strong illustration for *each* of the main truths he presents. In fact, no sermon is adequately prepared until such illustrations have been prayed over and planned for use. Never forget that illustrations are absolute necessities, not just decorative extras.

In Jesus' case, the parables served as His primary illustrations, and He depended heavily upon them. Matthew 13:34,35 tells us that for at least part of His ministry He taught only with parables. "...And without a parable spake he not unto them: *That it might be fulfilled which was spoken by the prophet, saying, I will open my mouth in parables; I will utter things which have been kept secret from the foundation of the world.*" This is a very strong statement in support of sermon illustrations because it appears that if Jesus did not have an illustration to make His point, He didn't even try to make it.

When Jesus was asked, *Who is my neighbor?* (Luke 10:29), He could have answered by giving a good, accurate definition such as: "A neighbor is anyone who needs your help and who is within your capacity to help." But of course He didn't answer that way. Instead He responded: *A certain man went down from Jerusalem to Jericho, and fell among thieves.* And you hear the exciting cops-and-robbers sort of story we call "The Good Samaritan."

Jesus knew that people don't generally get as much from a definition as from an example. His story made the answer so clear to the man who initially asked the neighbor question that there was no doubt in his mind concerning "who his neighbor was" when the teaching was done.

## Where to find illustration material

You *must* have an illustration to get an idea across effectively. But to use one, you must have one, and this is one of the most difficult problems for any speaker. The trouble is, an illustration cannot be produced at will just when you need one. Various other sermon elements such as the basic research, proposition statement, and outline can be created simply by taking the time to do the work. But an illustration is different. You can't make an appointment with yourself for a particular time to produce an illustration.

A good preacher is continuously watching for illustrations as he goes about his daily affairs. You will want to look for illustrations of all kinds of truth, not just on the subject you expect to preach on the following Sunday.

You can get them from:

- What you read

- What you see

- What you hear

- What you experience

There are many good second-hand illustrations available in books. But the best sermon illustrations come from sources close to you because of the accuracy and reality with which you can tell your own experience. Be continuously alert to possible illustrations. Always carry pen and paper so you can capture them when they unexpectedly appear.

Remember, an illustration must create a picture in the mind of the listener. Its power and effectiveness will be in proportion to the vividness of the picture it creates and the feelings it evokes.

At the point of using an illustration, you have two choices:

1. Make the point, then give the illustration.

2. Give the illustration, then make the point.

The first way is the safest way, especially if you are still developing your illustration-telling skills. If you tell the illustration without the audience knowing your sermon point, there is a danger that they will be listening for the wrong thing as you continue and derive something you did not intend. However, if you

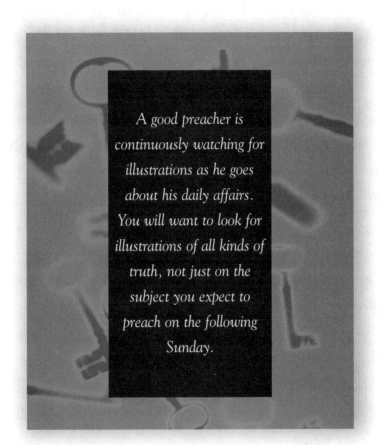

*A good preacher is continuously watching for illustrations as he goes about his daily affairs. You will want to look for illustrations of all kinds of truth, not just on the subject you expect to preach on the following Sunday.*

are adept at telling illustration stories and you have a strong illustration that opens the hearer's imagination window, it may have more power up front if you let it make its own point. Just tell it.

## Context

By "context" we mean the total cultural, situational, and literary environment of a passage of Scripture. We will understand

the meaning better if we consider all the circumstances sur-
rounding the "text" itself. In other worlds, it isn't enough just to
know the meaning of the words — we must also understand how
and why these words were used in each specific situation.

For example, several passages in the Bible contain the
three important words, *faith, hope,* and *love,* but the passages do
not always list them in the same order. Why would this be? The
*context* explains it.

In Hebrews 6, verses 10-12, the sequence is
"love...hope...faith," as if faith is the most climactic of the
three. This emphasis on faith is a natural quality of Hebrews.
(We call Hebrews 11 the "faith chapter" of the Bible.)

However, in 1 Thessalonians 1:3, the same words are in a
different sequence, "faith...love...hope." This appears to be
because the emphasis of the book is Christ's second coming,
which is the believer's great hope. Hope is therefore the climax
of the series.

Then in 1 Corinthians 13:13, the order of the words is
"faith...hope...love," because Paul wants us to see that love is
the greatest. The whole subject of the chapter is love.

This does not mean that wherever there is a sequence, the
final item is always the most important. But it does mean that
in Scripture — as in all literature — the fine points of the
meaning often depend upon our understanding the context.

Any Scripture taken "out of context" may easily be misunderstood or distorted.

## Exposition

The exposition of Scripture involves explaining the implications of a text that go beyond the words of a passage in order to apply the Bible's principles to everyday life. Exposition discloses the true meaning of a portion of the Bible, so this is certainly one of the highest, most important goals of good preaching.

## Exhortation

To exhort is to urge by admonition or imperative the Bible's truth in the form of command: "Love one another!" "Have faith!" "Repent!"

Exhortation is one of the most basic meanings of preaching, but it should be balanced with other qualities. A preacher who does nothing but "give orders" in his preaching may seem to be continuously scourging his congregation. So you will usually do better to offer your exhortation with love and tenderness, instead of fiery threats of judgment.

## Content

The content of a sermon refers to the meat of the message's *ideas* and *truth* regardless of the delivery style or illustrations used to preach it. Content is the cargo, not the vehicle. A speaker may have a beautiful, attractive style, but have nothing important to say, so solid God-given content is the starting point when preparing any sermon.

## Delivery

Finally, delivery is the way a sermon is presented. It is the preacher's technique, distinct from content. Delivery is the vehicle of voice, bodily movement, eyes, gestures, style, etc., that conveys the message. Once the preacher has good "content" to convey, he must match its quality with equally good delivery to get his message across. It is a common but serious mistake in preaching to assume that if the content is excellent, the delivery doesn't really matter. Nothing could be further from the truth, because it is often the form of delivery that will most determine how the message is received by an audience.

Now let's start getting organized in chapter 6.

# CHAPTER SIX

# HOW IS A SERMON ORGANIZED?

The simplest structure concept of any sermon (or speech) is actually an automatic one. Every oral presentation has these parts:

*The introduction*. This is the way you begin, and you must begin one way or another. So, whether graceful or not, you have an introduction.

*The body*. This is the meat of a sermon's message. The body contains the thing or things you stood up to say. And you must

have had something in mind that needed saying, or you would not have stood up — right? So your message has a body, beautiful or otherwise.

*The conclusion.* This is how a sermon ends, whether sooner...or later. It may be an eloquent crescendo, or it may be completely unplanned, but a conclusion must come, for better or worse.

If left to chance, none of these three sermon parts will be very satisfying to the speaker or the audience. Elsewhere in this manual, I suggest some things these parts should contain. To summarize:

The introduction serves the function of capturing the attention of the audience and connecting with their interests. A good introduction makes people want to listen.

The conclusion serves the function of suggesting an appropriate response on the part of the audience. A successful conclusion causes people to seek ways to apply your message to their personal lives.

That leaves the body of the sermon for consideration. The body contains the main ideas you are trying to get across, so it is a good idea to first make a list of these ideas. Next, note beside each one a reminder of the strong illustration you will use to "drive the point home." Once you have done this —

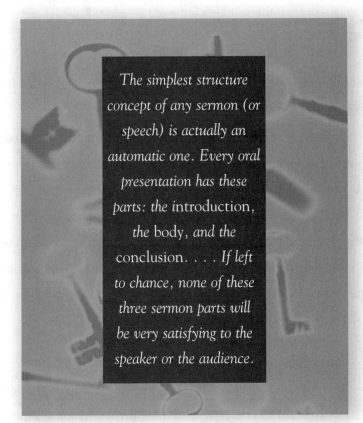

*The simplest structure concept of any sermon (or speech) is actually an automatic one. Every oral presentation has these parts: the* introduction, the body, *and the* conclusion. . . . *If left to chance, none of these three sermon parts will be very satisfying to the speaker or the audience.*

*voila!* — you have a sermon outline! I know it is easier said than done, but this is the primary way to think of sermon structure.

Remember, preaching without a clear structure (outline) is like handing those twenty eggs to your listeners, one after the other. When you pass truth out in such a way, you make it

impossible for the audience to gather it and take it home. *Structure* is the basket you give them to carry the eggs away safely.

Good *illustrations* help your listeners remember individual points, but it is the *structure* in a sermon's body that helps them remember the sermon as a whole.

Therefore, it is not particularly important from the listener's point of view that your structure outline be particularly neat or beautiful. It is simply a list of the main ideas of your sermon. But the strength of your sermon will depend largely upon the strength of the list — so make it memorable! If you end up with all style and no substance, you may dazzle your listeners with some fancy footwork, but the message you leave with them will probably be forgotten before the day's end.

## Sermon Classification

Sermons may usefully be classified according to the *source* of their structure. The following classifications are commonly used.

**1. A textual sermon** is one in which main divisions are derived directly from clear points or divisions in the Bible text itself.

**Example:**

**TEXT:** Micah 6:8 — *"What does the Lord require of us?"*

1....*to do justly...*

2.*...to love mercy...*

3.*...to walk humbly...*

The sermon's list of ideas is:

• Justice

• Mercy

• Humility

The list in this type of sermon is obviously taken directly from the elements named in the verse. A sermon organized in this way is called a *textual sermon.*

**2. A topical sermon** is organized by logical divisions of the subject, rather than divisions of the text.

**Example:**

**TEXT:** John 3:16 — *For God so loved the world....*

**SUBJECT:** Love

• Sensual love

• Brotherly love

• Divine love

This list is purely topical. The chosen sermon will deal with "three kinds of love," although only divine love is mentioned in the text. A sermon organized in this way is called a *topical sermon.*

Either of these common structures can be the basis of a fine sermon. Topical sermons are the more common form, but in my opinion it is simply because this form is somewhat easier to prepare without digging deeply into Scripture. Textual sermons have the greatest potential for powerful impression because they deal with ideas actually listed in the text, and are therefore less subject to the whims and prejudices of the preacher. But this does not mean that topical sermons are bad or should be avoided.

It is also possible for a sermon outline to be a compromise between the two forms, using divisions which are suggested only vaguely in the text but made into logical points by the preacher. Some textbooks refer to this kind of sermon as *textual-topical*.

**3. An expository sermon** is a textual sermon, but one with certain additional characteristics. Besides having a structure clearly taken from the text, it will usually be:

• Based on a longer passage of Scripture than the average text.

• Dependent on a deeper than usual exposition that probes for meanings not obvious to the casual Bible reader.

Always keep in mind that some kind of identifiable structure is always necessary to ensure that a sermon will make an impact and be remembered by the listener.

An *illustration* helps the listener remember one certain truth.

An *outline* (*structure*) gives memorability to the entire message.

Once the preacher's outline has been tentatively decided, it should be checked to ensure that it contains the elements to appeal to the three parts of human personality — intellect, emotions, and will.

In the Micah 6:8 passage, for instance, all three appeals are present:

To the *intellect:* The *logic* of justice.

To the *emotions:* The *compassion* of mercy.

To the *will:* The *choice* of unselfishness.

These three elements make up a kind of psychological sermon outline. These elements are not absolute necessities, but using them is usually a good idea. They may not always be in balance, and now and then one or the other may be missing — but they provide a valuable checklist for critiquing your sermon before you preach it. Are you giving your listeners something to *think,* something to *feel,* and something to *decide?*

There are endless possibilities as to the *form* of a sermon outline. Again, it is just a *list* of ideas, and doesn't need to be a scholarly analysis. But its divisions (points) are more useful if they share one or more of the following qualities:

*Novelty* — unusual choice of word or words.

*Alliteration* — all main points using the same initial letter.

*Parallel grammatical structure* — all points consisting of the same part of speech (e.g., all nouns, all verbal expressions, all adjectives).

*Parallel importance* — no one point overwhelmingly more vital than the others.

*Logical order* — including:

- Ascending order of importance

- Chronological order

- Cause-and-effect order

- Simple-to-difficult order

Sometimes there is good reason to present your list of thoughts in a different order than the order used in the text. For example: In Psalm 1, the godly man is described first, then the ungodly. But for preaching purposes you might want to reverse the order to end up on a more positive note.

Finally, it is not wise to force or distort the ideas of your message to merely give it a catchy outline of alliteration or novelty. But if you can give your main points some labels that are easily remembered, so much the better.

# CHAPTER SEVEN

# HOW DO I PREPARE?

We can classify sermon preparation in several ways. For example, there is *spiritual* preparation and *technical* preparation. Some preachers neglect one or the other, but both deserve careful attention because *balance* is needed. To ensure a good balance, both general and specific guidelines are necessary in the preparation process.

## General Preparation

General preparation involves the sum total of one's background experience, including previous sermons. You can probably

---

think of a subject or a text you know so well you could deliver a sermon on it with little preparation. You would want to call upon this knowledge when making general preparation for a sermon that deals with that subject.

## Specific Preparation

Specific preparation is the additional effort required to get ready for a preaching engagement at a certain time and place. It is the kind of effort you would make if you were scheduled to speak to a church group or conference tomorrow.

These two kinds of preparation can be compared to money in the bank and money in your pocket. When you have prepared to preach for a particular occasion, it is like earning pocket money. But when your message has been delivered, the preparations you made ahead of time are automatically deposited in an "account" of general preparation from which you can draw material for future sermons. Beginning preachers must "earn" their way by spending more time in specific preparations, while experienced preachers have more material in their deposit of general preparations.

A common temptation for the experienced minister as he grows older, however, is to depend too much on his general deposit, which makes his preaching stale. Every sermon deserves specific preparation.

Divine guidance is the first and greatest need in the preparation of a message. When you allow the inspiration of God to decide your subject, His blessing will be built into it. Asking for His blessing only after making all your own decisions is risky. This doesn't mean you must have some spectacular or supernatural revelation to tell you what to say. God's guidance for a preacher is much like His guidance for any other sincere believer — it comes in different ways. In Chapter 11 you will find some suggestions as to sources of sermon subjects. While God may use these, He certainly isn't limited to them.

Beyond spiritual readiness through prayer, some of a preacher's most practical tools of preparation include:

## The Bible

This is the single most important tool of any Christian minister during sermon preparation. Every preacher and Bible teacher should be a collector of Bibles. There are many English Bible versions available, and your collection should include several. Use them as part of your sermon preparation, by looking up your text in more than one version. Differing Hebrew and Greek translations often add depth and color to a passage of Scripture. If a preacher is bi- or even multi-lingual, he should have Bible translations in as many foreign languages as he is able to read.

Without making a detailed comparison of the various versions, it is enough to say that the Bible you use for your "recreational reading" may not be the best one to preach from. Some of the more modern versions are paraphrases that strive to translate "cultural equivalents" rather than literal meanings. This is a valid approach to Bible translation as far as giving the feel and the sense of a passage. But preaching from such a version is risky because you may be basing some of your main points on meanings that are not actually in the original text.

Some versions of the Bible make it easier to find structure that lends itself to  making a textual outline. The King James or the New King James versions are good in this regard. Other versions are equally accurate, but may sometimes minimize the structure for the sake of smooth reading.

Never be afraid to write notes and reminders in the margins of your Bible. Underlining, circling, highlighting, and noting cross-references will greatly increase your Bible's usefulness, especially for preaching or teaching.

## A System of Accumulation

To take full advantage of your "deposit" of general preparations you need to set up a system for information storing that allows you to easily and quickly retrieve your notes when you need them again. I don't call it a filing system because that suggests something rather complex. Keep it simple. Elaborate files

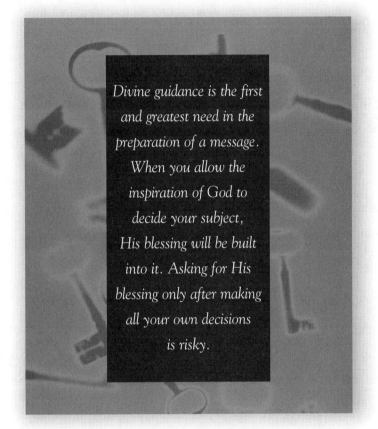

Divine guidance is the first
and greatest need in the
preparation of a message.
When you allow the
inspiration of God to
decide your subject,
His blessing will be built
into it. Asking for His
blessing only after making
all your own decisions
is risky.

are more a hindrance than a help. Many preachers have ministered successfully for years using nothing more complicated than a shoe box or some other small container to hold their notes of outlines and illustrations.

When you need to prepare a sermon, start with your collection of resource material. You will often find something useful

that can be combined with new material to create new notes. Then, after you have preached that sermon, add your new outline notes to your collection for later reference.

If it ever becomes necessary to have a more conventional filing system (perhaps after several years), keep it as simple as possible. Many preachers have valuable material filed in such a way that they can't find it when they need it. It is best to file material under headings that have to do with a sermon's probable *use*, not its source. Don't have a file marked "Time Magazine" or "News Items." But do have "Easter Material" and "Youth Meetings."

## The Bible Concordance

A concordance is a list of words found in some version of the Bible. Each occurrence of a word is identified by a Scripture reference. Concordance words are listed alphabetically and are normally included in a sentence fragment that shows its contextual use.

Obviously, some common words like "and" or "the" occur hundreds or even thousands of times. These and other words that are not perceived to have any doctrinal significance may not be included in some concordances. The problem is determining which words should be included and which should be omitted. In making this decision, some concordances (especially those found in the backs of Bibles) may list only "important" words. Using

such concordances can be frustrating because they often ignore the subject or word you are seeking to find.

## The Exhaustive Bible Concordance

An exhaustive or "complete" concordance includes every occurrence of every word found in Scripture. This is a preparation tool that any serious preacher should have in his/her library. The exhaustive concordance also incorporates Hebrew and Greek translations, thus providing more detailed insight as to the intended meaning.

For example, before you preach on "hell" from a certain passage, you will want to check your concordance to see whether the true meaning of the word translated in that passage is actually *grave* (Hades), or *lake of fire* (Gehenna).

Here are some other ways an exhaustive Bible concordance can help a preacher:

- Shows the distribution of certain themes throughout the Bible.

- Finds passages that repeat an idea.

- Finds an entire passage when only a fragment is remembered — by searching for key words.

- Shows nuances of meaning by revealing every context in which a certain word is used.

- Traces the historical origin of a word and its relatives.

## The Bible Dictionary

The Bible dictionary is another vital research tool for any practicing preacher. It is most valuable for checking words which you suspect may have a specialized meaning. Structured much like a general information encyclopedia, this study tool supplies working definitions of Bible terms, including their cultural, historical, and linguistic backgrounds.

## Commentaries

A commentary is simply a set of written comments of explanation or analysis on various Bible passages. No commentary tries to deal with every single verse of the Bible. Many even seem to omit comment on difficult passages where you most need help and go into too much depth on obvious passages. But they can be helpful in improving the depth of your message at times, so having them available can be an advantage.

Huge expensive sets of commentaries, however, are usually not worth the money. A one-volume commentary on an individual Bible book is usually of better quality because it was probably written by someone who spent years studying that particular book. No one can be equally authoritative about the entire Bible.

Just remember that any commentary is naturally colored by the theological stance of the commentator. Scholars and teachers who write them range from radically *liberal* to narrowly

*fundamental.* So remember — your own Spirit-led interpretation may be better.

## Personal Observation for Illustrations

As I pointed out in Chapter 6, direct experiences of life are the *best* sources for illustrations. But you can also glean vicariously from what you read or observe in the lives of others. Finding an illustration can't be planned. It must be seized as it appears. A preacher must watch for scenes and events in daily life that will help him create mental pictures for his listeners.

## Meditation

This could be called the "dog-bone method" of Bible study, because in the meditation process you spiritually "chew" on a passage repeatedly. Joshua was commanded to meditate on God's Word in Joshua 1:8 to ensure Israel's covenant obedience and good success. Paul likened the process in Colossians 3:16 to letting ...*the word of Christ dwell in you richly....* Meditation is simply an intense or prolonged pondering upon a portion of Scripture.

Asking yourself every question you can imagine about the context of a passage when meditating can be very helpful in expanding your understanding. Some questions you will always want to ask include: Who did it? Who said it? Why did they do or say it? Who else was there? What attitudes were shown?

What was the history of the event? Are there other similar places in the Bible? Hundreds of other questions are possible. So ask them, because questioning the context of Scripture is an important way of receiving revelation.

## Discipline

Preparation for preaching is serious business and is not to be taken lightly. So let me give you a few practical rules of behavior — beyond actual sermon preparation — which will help *you* prepare to be at your best.

First, don't eat a heavy meal just before a service. This well-known behavior principle has always applied to preparing for strenuous physical or mental activity. But it also applies to the physical and mental activity of preaching.

Preachers have an extra temptation in this area, because they are often invited to  special dinners just before a meeting. Decline gracefully if you can, but at the very least, eat only a very small quantity of light food.

Also use discipline in taking special care to avoid emotionally stressful situations during the hours just before you are to preach. (When we are driving to church, my wife does *not* use that time to tell me about the breakdown of the washing machine or the kids' fight with the neighbors.) If necessary, ask for the cooperation of family members to help you avoid controversies, upsetting news, critical decisions, and noisy social

occasions. You need quiet time when you are nearing your time of delivery, not conversation. Solitude is a necessary ingredient of sermon preparation, so ask your family to help you in this area when your pulpit time draws near.

And above all, pray for God's presence, direction, and sermon selection as you prepare to preach His will.

# CHAPTER EIGHT

# HOW DO I SOUND?

**O**nce you feel you have been entrusted with a message from God, equipped it with potent illustrations, and structured it in an effective form, there still remains the issue of getting it planted in the hearts and minds of the listeners. This is the *delivery* of your sermon. So in this chapter we will consider the basic tool a preacher uses to get his message across to the listeners — the voice.

## Voice

The human voice is the sermon delivery's most vital tool, but it is often the most neglected. Unfortunately, the technology of microphones and amplifiers has given many preachers the impression that any kind of talking will do. Somehow, in some preachers' thinking, the public address system can take care of poor voice inflection and enunciation. However, poor speech cannot be transformed into good speech by amplifying it through expensive equipment. It simply becomes *loud poor speech* — which more people can hear because of the equipment.

A good preacher really shouldn't need an amplifier except for audiences of three hundred or more. Jesus spoke to five thousand without amplification. John Wesley and George Whitefield had no giant Bose or Peavey loudspeakers to help them when they addressed crowds of up to fifty thousand. I am not suggesting that you should try to do the same. I simply want to point out that over-dependence on electronic equipment can diminish the effectiveness of your sermon delivery.

Properly used, your voice can become strong enough to fill a sizeable room — but it will never develop unless you challenge it to carry farther than your microphone stand.

The human voice is a delicate yet powerful instrument of infinite variety. It can convey feeling and expression far beyond

the simple meaning of spoken words. And you have a great degree of control over how your voice sounds. Although you inherit the physical characteristics of your vocal mechanism, you can, by practice and attention, modify and improve your voice considerably.

Voice production is actually a muscular activity. Like any such activity, it can benefit by careful exercise. You can control and modify your voice production in the following five ways:

### Pitch

Pitch is a musical term that refers to the relative position of a tone — either high or low — on the musical scale. You may be a bass or a soprano, but within your own voice range, you can still choose to go high, low, or in between. The same is true for talking because your speaking voice also has a pitch.

The difference between singing and talking is exactly that, when singing, a pitch is maintained long enough to be identifiable. When speaking, pitch moves up and down too rapidly to be identified, even on a single syllable.

For a public speaker, two principles of pitch are in conflict with each other:

High pitch carries over greater distance with less effort.

Low pitch is more pleasant and less tiring for the listener.

An overwhelming majority of professional speakers (radio announcers, newscasters, actors), whether men or women, are hired because of their low-pitched voices simply because people find them more pleasant to listen to. There is a scientific reason for this: In civilization (and nature), high-pitched sounds tend to be associated with trauma and pain. A scream of terror is high-pitched, as is the cry of a wounded animal. The shattering of glass, the screech of brakes, and the crash of metal when cars collide are all high-pitched noises. Therefore, the human subconscious associates high vocal sounds with stress and unpleasantness.

This is hardly the feeling you want to give your audience. Therefore, when preaching, you should use mostly the lower half of your vocal range. Use the upper range only for occasional variety or contrast, or when it is difficult to be heard. Do *not* — as so many barnstorming preachers do — shriek at a high pitch for minutes at a time, thinking it is more effective or that it represents special anointing.

How can you find your best level of pitch? Go to a piano and identify the highest and lowest notes you can comfortably sing. Then find the mid-point between the two. Now move lower (left) a few notes from that point. Right there is probably the best-sounding area of pitch for your particular voice.

> A scream of terror is high-pitched, as is the cry of a wounded animal. The shattering of glass, the screech of brakes, and the crash of metal when cars collide are all high-pitched noises. Therefore, the human subconscious associates high vocal sounds with stress and unpleasantness. This is hardly the feeling you want to give your audience.

## Loudness

Loudness is the range of amplitude or volume of any tone or noise. It is controllable entirely apart from pitch, although we tend to mix the two together, going high and loud or low and soft. But it is quite possible — and sometimes desirable — to be high and soft or low and loud.

The general rule for loudness is this: Use a level somewhat louder than necessary but not three times louder. There are several good reasons for this.

First, for the benefit of people with hearing impairment, you need to speak a bit louder than normal. A little extra volume allows them to hear you more comfortably and gives them access to the truth you are preaching.

Also, in any audience, there is likely to be some interference, whether sporadic or continuous. The noise of an air conditioner or a passing car competes with the speaker's voice, and an occasional cough blots out a word here and there. To overcome these handicaps, it is a good idea to speak a little louder than what is absolutely necessary. It will help you if you always think in terms of speaking to the *back* rows, not the front.

## Rate

Rate refers to the speed of speech in words per minute. It is controlled in two ways:

1. The use of pauses between words.

2. The rate at which the actual enunciation takes place.

Silence, in small segments, is not necessarily a speaker's enemy. One of the most persistent of bad habits is the practice of filling any blank spot with "...and...," "...uh...," or "...er...." Books on public speaking sometimes call these kinds of meaningless expressions, "whangdoodles." Just as bad are trite

expressions used (often unconsciously) over and over again, such as, "you know...," "I mean...," "okay...," or "you see...."

Many factors may dictate a speaker's choice of speaking rate, but one universal principle is this generality: The larger the audience, the slower the rate the speaker should use.

Slowing the rate in larger listening audiences has to do primarily with the problem of interference. If ten people in an audience of one hundred have coughs, that means thirty people in an audience of three hundred will have coughs. And every cough wipes out the speaker's voice for a little circle of listeners who are seated around the one with the cough. Slowing your delivery means fewer words are wiped out. You give the distracted listeners additional leeway to keep up with your points in between all the coughs.

Also, if the speaker is talking very rapidly, the audience is not as careful to be quiet. There will be more movement in and out, more crying babies, and even conversations. So remember — the larger the audience, the more slowly you speak.

## Tone quality

This hard-to-define element is mostly hereditary. Tone quality is the unique pattern of undertones and overtones (harmonics) that identifies one person's voice from someone else's. Most of us have only limited control of our tone quality.

Listen to yourself, and simply strive for a smooth, pleasant sound. Avoid harshness, hoarseness, and nasality.

## Articulation

The complex movements and placements of the whole vocal mechanism constitute a person's articulation. Our vocal cords, throat surface, soft palate, uvula, tongue, lips, teeth, and jaws are all movable to one degree or another. It is the placement of these parts in a huge variety of relative positions that creates the speech sounds we produce.

There are more than twelve hundred different speech sounds in use in all the languages of the world combined. A single language uses perhaps fifty or sixty of them. English uses only forty-four. Yet any voice is capable of producing all twelve hundred of them.

Phonetics is the science of speech sounds. Its study can help a person overcome any defective pronunciation or imitate any "accent." If you are aware of any articulatory problem and you are serious about preaching, you can cure the difficulty if you are willing to get the help of a voice coach and work hard. Speech habits are years old, and are hard to break.

We often use two specialized terms related to articulation:

*Pronunciation* is a speaker's concept of how a word should be said...the intended sound.

*Enunciation* refers to how clearly he articulates his intended sounds. The general rule is: Don't be afraid to open your mouth when you speak!

There is no substitute for clear speech. Your ideas may be sensational, your motivation sincere, and your preparation impeccable, but if you don't speak plainly, it will all be lost. Your voice is the final link between your message and the congregation.

# CHAPTER NINE

# HOW DO I LOOK?

**A**lthough the voice is the most important tool of delivery, it is certainly not the only tool God has given us to aid in preaching His truth. We all know that hearing a message on a cassette is not the same as hearing it in person. The difference is largely because all the visual elements of communication are missing from an audio recording. Your presence as a preacher has as much to do with projecting your message as a clear articulate voice. The following are some valuable non-vocal tools you will want to use.

## Eyes

Your eyes are the most expressive part of your face — and the most watched by an audience. If we were rating these "tools" that God has equipped you with to preach, your eyes would be second in importance only to your voice. Properly used, your eyes can add much to the effectiveness of your preaching. Improperly used, they can be a handicap.

Actors use eye makeup, not to be more attractive but to make the expression of their eyes more visible. You may not use makeup, but there are other important ways to maintain good eye visibility. Eyeglasses are a barrier. Preach without them if you can. And sunglasses are much worse.

Because your eyes are so visible, make sure that you use them to the fullest effect as communication tools. Consider the following do's and don'ts of using your eyes in the public speaking environment.

## Some Don'ts

DON'T stare at the floor, out the window, or at a spot on the wall. You may feel it helps control your fright or makes you appear meditative, but your audience will think you are trying avoid them. You are speaking to the people, so look at the people.

DON'T look only at friends or important people. Every speaker likes to get reinforcement and approval from his audience, so the tendency is to look for it from friends or those in authority. But an audience picks up on this quickly and feels disengaged because they're "left out." So take in everyone.

DON'T turn and look at anyone who may be seated on the platform behind you, no matter how important they are. They know and understand that the audience in front of you must be your focus. So look at those you came to minister to. Engage God's sheep who came to be fed.

DON'T close your eyes for long periods of time. This is a bad habit of many gospel singers that has carried over to some preachers. It may make you seem worshipful, but it makes an audience feel left out.

DON'T look at the source of disturbances that may occur. Any late entrance, exit, or surprise noise will distract some of your audience — but the surest way to let it distract *all* of them is to allow it to distract you. Ignore it and stay focused.

## Some Do's

DO make brief eye contact over the entire audience, including those who may be at the extreme left or right.

DO look most of the time at those people who are farthest away from you. Let your eyes sweep left and right along the *back* row, not the front. Your line of sight creates a sort of invisible plane going out from you to the audience. If you look at the back row, those in front will feel included. But if you look only at those seated in front, those behind will feel excluded.

DO look up from your Bible or notes to make eye contact with the audience as much as possible. Even while reading your text, the best technique is to keep a finger on your place, read a verse silently, and then look up at the audience while you speak it. With a bit of practice this becomes quite natural, and can be done without long gaps or pauses.

## Posture

Good posture is very important in the pulpit. A speaker should have an alert, energetic appearance. You can achieve this in large part by keeping your body weight forward on your toes, not on your heels. Stand in such a way that at any time it would be possible to actually rise on your toes without losing your balance. "Stay on your toes" is good advice not only for athletes but also for speakers. Not only will you look more alert, but some of the dynamism will often come through in your voice.

The most useful position for your feet during public speaking is to place them apart leaving just enough room for an extra shoe in between. Modeling schools instruct young ladies to keep their feet entirely together when standing, preferably with the heel of one pressed against the instep of the other, and at a

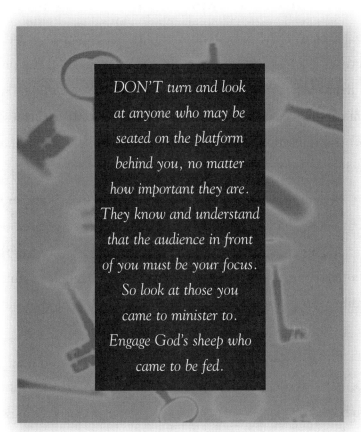

DON'T *turn and look at anyone who may be seated on the platform behind you, no matter how important they are. They know and understand that the audience in front of you must be your focus. So look at those you came to minister to. Engage God's sheep who came to be fed.*

slightly toes-out angle. This position certainly makes most women appear more graceful. But preaching is not charm school, and for mobility and stability a speaker needs a slightly stronger stance.

The other extreme is standing with legs wide apart, as if on the deck of a rolling ship. Don't do it.

## Movement

Except in the more formal, traditional churches, preachers are no longer expected to remain stationary behind the pulpit to deliver their sermons. Some may still prefer to do so, and some audiences may expect it. Where an amplifier is necessary and the microphone is fastened solidly to the pulpit, there is hardly an alternative.

Where it is possible and acceptable, however, some movement is usually desirable when preaching. One simple reason is that an audience gives better attention to a moving object than to a fixed one, and maintaining visual attention helps maintain auditory attention. But more important is the fact that movement can be used to enhance and strengthen the message.

To accomplish this, movement must not be aimless, but should be related to meaning or mood. Taking a new position as you begin to talk about a new idea is a way of giving your message a "fresh start." When you move to a different spot, the listener turns his head slightly to follow you. This marks a small change for him, and a renewal of attention. He now sees you against a slightly different background than before, giving the freshness of variety.

Move when you start a new idea, give an illustration, or give your subject new emphasis. Don't simply pace back and forth, turning only when you reach an obstacle (like the end of

the platform). This "caged animal" kind of movement adds nothing to your effectiveness.

Studies of "audience attention span" tell us a speaker needs to recapture attention every few minutes. Bodily movement, if coordinated with your message content, can help accomplish this.

## Hands and Gestures

Be conscious of what the audience sees you doing with your hands. If you can rest your hands on a pulpit or hold a Bible when you speak, it may solve the problem of what to do with your hands. But if you aren't holding a Bible (or notes) and there is nothing separating you from the audience, then what?

Some public speaking textbooks advise you to let your hands hang loosely at your sides. But very few speakers can do this without feeling terribly awkward. For most people a better idea is to keep the elbows somewhat bent, and the hands near each other in front of the body. The hands may be touching or nearly touching each other. This is general advice in normal circumstances — not a position that must be rigidly maintained. Do what feels comfortable as long as it doesn't look bizarre to the audience.

As for the position of the hands themselves, a sort of pen-holding position is most natural for most speakers. When a hand is held flat, it looks awkward. When clenched, a hand

looks threatening. So hold either hand as if you were about to write with an invisible pen. You will seem relaxed and reasonably graceful.

Don't keep your hands clasped behind your back! This will cause your shoulders to rotate and slightly compress your chest, making breathing a bit more difficult. You don't need the handicap. Opera singers always keep their hands well in front of their bodies, often pressing against each other. Why? Because it helps their breath control. Experienced professional speakers and singers *never* clasp their hands behind their backs for more than a few seconds at a time. Follow their example.

Don't speak with your hands near your face, particularly near your mouth. You will appear self-conscious and may create a physical obstacle for the projection of your voice.

## Gestures

Like bodily movements, hand movements (gestures) can help or hinder a sermon. And gestures, like words, are a language. As a language, they are part of a culture, and have different meanings to different people. It is therefore good to understand that certain gestures may be interpreted in a variety of ways. What is "cute" in one culture may be obscene in another. It is not possible to identify and prescribe certain gestures that are suitable universally.

The main idea of a gesture is to coordinate it with the thought that is being expressed. Shakespeare said, "Suit the action to the word, the word to the action." This is still good advice. When you are presenting a sweeping thought, add to your thought a sweeping gesture. When presenting a stingy thought, present it with a stingy gesture. Don't gesture just to be moving. Movement must mean something.

A speaker has an increasing problem of holding visual attention as audience size increases. So when preaching to larger crowds, increase the size of your gestures to help them stay focused. A general rule to remember is: the larger the audience, the larger the appropriate gesture.

Finally, some gestures easily become habitual. So watch — and ask others to watch — for any tendencies you may have to over-do any hand movements, because meaningless movement can be distracting. Tugging at a belt or an earlobe, clasping your hands, running your hand through your hair, pointing nowhere with a forefinger, loosening an already-loose collar, scratching an imaginary itch — such idiosyncrasies can become easily embedded in a preaching style.

The final measure of worth for any gesture is: Does it help? If not, it is better to discard it.

# CHAPTER TEN

# AM I ANOINTED?

**S**o far I have given you many keys that make for better preaching. Now, as we near the end of this text, I want to remind you of three absolutely indispensable keys or elements that make up an effective sermon:

VIVID ILLUSTRATIONS — Those very necessary windows for the truth.

MEMORABLE STRUCTURE — That very necessary "basket" in which the listener can carry the truth home.

THE TOUCH OF GOD — The vital element that makes a sermon not a speech, but a message.

Any sermon that contains these three qualities is guaranteed to help someone. Any sermon missing any one of the three may or may not be helpful. In this chapter, I want to examine the last of these three primary keys: the touch of God. This element is a necessity because without the Holy Spirit's direction and inspiration, you only have a "speech."

The "touch of God," as I call it, is more commonly known as *inspiration* or *the anointing*. And if you have ever experienced it, whether in your own or someone else's ministry, you know it is real.

In this manual, we have dealt first with the matters of structure and illustrations, not because they are more important than God's anointing, but because young preachers so often think these techniques are unimportant. They feel that if they can just be spiritual enough, the elements of technique won't matter. But this is about as sensible as thinking that if you're spiritual enough, you will miraculously reach the church without the physical inconvenience of having to drive a car through traffic to get there. As one preaching authority has put it, "Anointed ignorance is still ignorance."

With that clearly said, let us quickly add that the touch of God is by far the most important element of any successful

sermon. It is true that many messages, sadly deficient in technique, have brought miracles and revival because of God's special presence. But think what they might have been if they had also had the bonus of good communication skills!

The late Brother J. C. Hibbard, who for more than thirty-five years pastored Gospel Lighthouse Church in Dallas, Texas, was a powerfully anointed if somewhat unpolished preacher. He never had the opportunity to study in a Bible school. His preaching skills (which, incidentally, demonstrated most of the principles discussed in this manual) were developed completely in the pulpit. And when all has been said, the pulpit is where your skills will be developed too.

Hibbard's wife, Nell, was a graduate of a well-known Bible college. She tells of a day in their early ministry when she volunteered to help J. C. prepare for his Sunday sermon with the aid of homiletic principles she had studied in college. He made his notes and tried his best to conform to the rules she explained to him. But for him, they didn't work. The armor wasn't a good fit (*see* 1 Samuel 17:38,39).

When Sunday came, Brother Hibbard's sermon turned out to be one of those that taxi down the runway forever but never make lift off. He was devastated, and drove home feeling like a failure. Nell tried to comfort him by pointing out some of the

brighter moments of the message, but she wasn't able to dispel his gloom.

Finally J. C. said, "Well, I'll tell you — if anybody got any good at all out of that message, *I* deserve all of the credit because the Lord never came anywhere near me while I was preaching it!" Many a preacher knows the misery of that feeling…and no one enjoys it. Brother Hibbard took stock of the homiletic principles his wife had shared, and started applying them in his own way, always seeking God's touch on the sermons. And Gospel Lighthouse Church was richly blessed by the result.

Since God's anointing is His own gift, there is no formula for obtaining it. He bestows it upon the simple as well as upon the learned. But there are some things you can do to make yourself a better candidate to receive His special touch.

**Prepare your heart.** Clear away, through repentance, any disobedience or rebellion within. Clear away, through forgiveness, any bad feelings toward others. Then preach only what you can feel deeply.

**Prepare your mind.** Give God the opportunity to plant His thoughts and message in your mind. When the thought of a sermon subject crosses your mind, go to the Bible and let Him guide you in developing its structure and aim. If you receive no

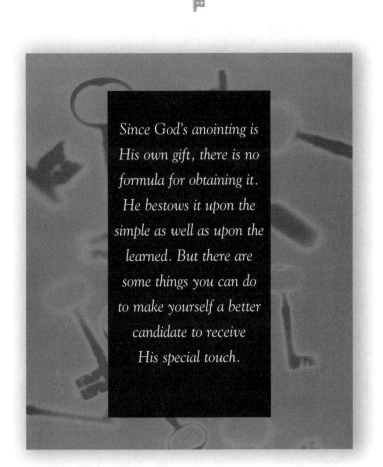

*Since God's anointing is His own gift, there is no formula for obtaining it. He bestows it upon the simple as well as upon the learned. But there are some things you can do to make yourself a better candidate to receive His special touch.*

direct instruction, use your own best godly judgment. When you ask for His touch, He will direct you.

**Prepare your sermon.** In the outline process, think through and pray over the list of ideas you are impressed to share. Dig for the right illustrations, plan your opening and closing, and make simple, careful notes.

**Prepare your physical body.** Get sufficient rest and don't overeat. Be neat and clean in body and clothing. Be at your best.

The powerful black poet James Weldon Johnson expresses a preacher's prayer in his poem, *God's Trombones*:

*"And now, O Lord, this man of God,*

*Who breaks the bread of life this morning —*

*Shadow him in the hollow of thy hand,*

*And keep him out of the gunshot of the devil.*

*Take him, Lord — this morning —*

*Wash him with hyssop inside and out,*

*Hang him up and drain him dry of sin,*

*Pin his ear to the wisdom-post,*

*And make his words sledgehammers of truth —*

*Beating on the iron heart of sin.*

*Lord God, this morning —*

*Put his eye to the telescope of eternity,*

*And let him look upon the paper walls of time.*

*Lord, turpentine his imagination,*

*Put perpetual motion in his arms,*

*Fill him full of the dynamite of thy power,*

*Anoint him all over with the oil of thy salvation,*

*And set his tongue on fire…"*

What an eloquent expression of a preacher's yearnings! May God answer that prayer for all of us!

The anointing is God's powerful presence. Despite the apparent opinions of some, it has nothing to do with:

| | |
|---|---|
| Loudness | Perspiration |
| Hoarseness | Long-windedness |
| Frenzy | Extravagant statements |
| Mysticism | Claims of infallibility |
| Personality | |

A divine anointing as it applies to preaching is simply the strong sense of the presence of God Himself in what is being said. It may be loud or quiet, exuberant or solemn, cheering or awesome. You can sometimes literally feel the anointing of God that is tangibly on His preaching servant. Sometimes the divine Presence is not so much upon the person as upon the words that go forth, zinging like arrows into listeners' hearts. Miraculous manifestations that follow the preaching of the Word are other proofs of God's tangible presence. He makes His presence known in different ways, and there is no substitute for it.

Finally, never think of God's anointing as some added blessing that is "poured" over your already-prepared message. Look for and pray for His anointing all the way through the sermon-development process. As you apply the good homiletic

techniques of this manual while allowing the Holy Spirit's shared input in the process, your sermon will be anointed. And people will be blessed.

One simple southern preacher gave this explanation of his sermon preparation procedure that invites God's touch: "First, I reads myself full; then I thinks myself clear; then I prays myself hot; then I just lets go!"

# CHAPTER ELEVEN

# WRAPPING THINGS UP —

## WATCHING THE CLOCK, VISUAL AIDS, AND MICROPHONES

**T**he more you preach, the better your preaching should become. And as you develop more experience, you will have less and less need to think about all the mechanical details we have talked about — where to look, how to stand, etc. Those aspects will become automatic, and you will be able to give full attention to your content, your choice of words, your delivery, and the voice of the Holy Spirit as to how you should conclude.

—

So be encouraged; preaching is not all a matter of following the rules of communication. But to improve steadily, you must be willing to give attention to smaller and smaller details — things that beginners don't think of at all. The inexorable "law of diminishing returns" means that to improve by ten percent, a good preacher must actually work much harder than a mediocre preacher. And that work is often done by simply observing miscellaneous tips that come from his own experience and the experience of others.

It is with some of these tips that we will conclude this manual.

## Respect the Clock!

The most common of preacher problems is preaching too long. So don't be a common preacher.

What power can the senses lull

As when a sermon, deadly dull,

Puts mind and body both to sleep

With thoughts that are more thick than deep!

So often, discourse meditative

Becomes instead just "sedative,"

While, droopy-eyed and dull of wit,

We have to sit, and sit, and sit…

Make sure a timepiece is where you can see it while speaking (without the audience's awareness that you are watching it). This may mean removing your wristwatch from your arm and placing it on the pulpit or lectern. *Don't* try to look at a wristwatch you are wearing while preaching. It is sure to make every listener refer to his own wristwatch, which will distract him and those sitting near him from hearing what you are saying.

Twenty minutes is considered the normal standard length for a Sunday morning sermon in most American "old-line" denominational churches. In some Independent, Charismatic, and enthusiastically Evangelical churches, the norm is longer — thirty minutes, forty-five minutes…even an hour. And there are some congregations in which time limits are unheard of. (These are the ones where only the fanatics return for the next meeting.)

Time is the most valuable commodity any human being possesses. So consider carefully your *audience expectations*. It is the preacher himself who usually has control over the length of his sermon, and far too many are undisciplined in fulfilling that responsibility. An anointed and well-prepared sermon can say more in ten minutes than an undisciplined stem-winder can say in two torturous hours.

Always consider the expectations of your listening audience. If a church has a long tradition of dismissing its Sunday

morning service at noon, their receptivity will be geared toward a noon sermon conclusion.

Some church workers will have planned Sunday afternoon outreach ministries that are scheduled to commence at 1:00, leaving them just enough time to get there if they leave the church by 12:05.

The children's church leaders expect to release the children at twelve.

The grouchy, unconverted husband of a godly little old lady expects to pick her up at the front door at twelve sharp.

The bus-riding family from the other side of town expects to catch their homeward-bound bus at 12:15.

And several families will always have Sunday roasts in self-timed ovens, set to be done at 12:20.

These considerations may not seem as important to you as taking the extra time for your inspiring message, but others may think otherwise. Would you like to be invited back to speak again? If so, respect the clock...and the people who depend upon it.

If you are a visiting speaker, never ask the pastor how long you should speak. Instead, ask what time the service usually ends. Also find out what, if anything, must be done at the close of the service after your message is over, and allow time for it. Then be sure you *stick to your time limits*.

> *It is the preacher himself who usually has control over the length of his sermon, and far too many are undisciplined in fulfilling that responsibility. An anointed and well-prepared sermon can say more in ten minutes than an undisciplined stem-winder can say in two torturous hours.*

Your topic was timely,

Your outline tip-top.

But please, may I give you a hint?

You came to so many

Good places to stop — but you din't!

## Visual Aids

Unfortunately, preachers have almost totally abandoned visual aids to the realm of teachers, and have cut themselves off from a great resource. People remember many times better what has been visually impressed.

True, most common preaching situations don't make it easy for the preacher to use visuals. There is nowhere to put a marker board where everyone can see it because there is a choir on the platform. Other people at the back of the hall are too far away to see what you're doing. So it is neither convenient nor graceful to carry your visuals onto the platform. I know all this — yet the fact remains that when you can manage it, visuals will almost always make your sermon more powerful.

If there is a *chalkboard* (or marker board), use it. But don't cover it with detailed material ahead of time. A chalkboard is most useful for things that are:

Simple — use single words, not sentences

Symbolic — use lines, arrows, circles

Simultaneous with speaking — do it while you talk

An *overhead projector* is a different thing. It is very difficult (though not impossible) to actually mark or change things while you speak. The acetate slides around, the marker turns out to be indelible, the room is too bright, the machine is on the wrong floor level, etc. An overhead's strongest use, therefore, is to

project prepared sermon material that merely needs to be laid in place.

Three-dimensional *objects* are probably the best choice for a preacher. They need not be spectacular. I have used an egg, a clock, a flowerpot, stuffed animals, candles, a pumpkin, a toy gun, a banana, a bundle of sticks, and a musical instrument, to name only a few. The idea is to focus audience attention and evoke a larger mental picture that illustrates your sermon points.

Don't make the mistake of thinking that visual aids are for use only with children. We are fooled into this belief because adults hide their boredom better than children do. When you lose a child's attention, you know it instantly because of the antics he starts. When you lose the adult's attention, he sits steady with that sweet smile of indulgence on his face — but his mind is on the golf course or at the dinner table.

Adult or child — give your listener something to look at when you can!

## How to End a Meeting

If you are a guest speaker, ending the meeting may not be your responsibility at all. You may be expected by the meeting host to simply conclude your message and sit down. But don't assume this. Consult with the pastor or whoever is in charge to understand the meeting's closing plan. He may want you to

oversee the altar call, then close the meeting himself with a special offering. You never know until you ask. So always ask.

The subject of altar calls is larger than I can deal with in detail in this manual, but here are some of the possibilities.

### Prayer

Prayer is always good follow-up for any message, even if the service is not yet ending. You might pray, asking God to plant the message in people's hearts. If the prayer is intended to mark the end of the meeting, make that clear before you begin to pray.

### Invitation

The nature of the invitation will depend upon the subject of the message. If you are inviting people to receive salvation, always provide easy-to-follow steps. Ask them to raise their hand, stand up, and come forward. This is a time-honored approach. You may be impressed to lead those who respond in a phrase-by-phrase prayer while they stand at the front. Or you may want to invite them to follow one of the counselors into a prayer room.

Always make sure that counselors and literature are available. There is nothing worse than a leader floundering in uncertainty when people are trying to make the most important decision of their lives!

### Music (congregation, choir, or musicians)

Music can be combined with an invitation. A spiritual music background invites a worshipful atmosphere and often makes it easier for some people to come forward.

## Plan!

Finally, the most important imperative for closing a meeting is to *plan!* All things are possible, but *plan!* You may come up with something better than anyone else has thought of yet, but *plan!* Then be willing to amend your plan if the Holy Spirit so leads. Unplanned conclusions tend to drag on forever in a series of post-script and last-minute ideas. Don't let it happen to you.

## How to Dress for Preaching

If your messages do their work entirely by means of audio-cassettes, what you wear when you record them obviously doesn't matter. But for most preachers, clothing does have an effect on the overall impact of the message. An extravagantly dressed preacher will not be very successful in preaching a message on "The Necessity of Sacrifice." Also, times change, and what is immodest in one generation may seem quite modest in the next. What always matters is the *listener's perception.*

You may be wearing a rhinestone, but if the audience thinks it is a five-carat diamond, it is judged accordingly. Dress conservatively. This does not mean you should always be the most formally dressed person present, but you certainly shouldn't be the most *informally* dressed. Try to dress just a bit more formally than the average person in the audience. This has to do with their perception of your respect for the occasion and for the Gospel.

As to colors, two contradictory principles have to be considered. Light colors hold an audience's attention more easily, especially in front of large crowds. (This is why big-time evangelists often wear white suits.) But dark colors project more sincerity and earnestness.

Although such perceptions vary with culture, studies have measured people's reactions to clothing and discovered that dark blue is generally perceived as the most "sincere" color for a man's suit. The least believable suit color is green, followed by chocolate brown.

The net result of such studies is that businessmen (including the Japanese) have adopted dark blue almost as a uniform. The other alternatives are black or gray, with beige a distant fourth. Not exactly a rainbow of choice, gentlemen.

The rules are broader for ladies and have more to do with style than color. However, it is worth pointing out that if immodesty is thought of as revealing the female form, very light colors are less modest than dark ones. This is because light-colored clothes make shadows, showing a sculpture of shape, whereas dark clothes cast no shadows and appear more formless. When you look at and consider a black sweater and a white sweater of the same design, the black will seem more modest.

It is worth noting that many experienced women preachers (Kathryn Kuhlman is one example) have preached in

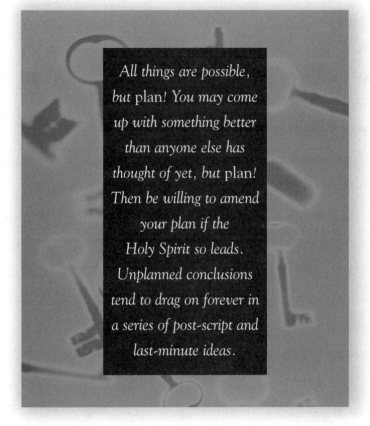

> *All things are possible,*
> *but* plan! *You may come*
> *up with something better*
> *than anyone else has*
> *thought of yet, but* plan!
> *Then be willing to amend*
> *your plan if the*
> *Holy Spirit so leads.*
> *Unplanned conclusions*
> *tend to drag on forever in*
> *a series of post-script and*
> *last-minute ideas.*

long-sleeved dresses. "Cap" sleeves or sleeveless dresses are not suitable for preaching, even in today's progressive cultures. So culture and modesty, more than color, have everything to do with dressing to present your message the best way.

For both men and women, it is a good idea to *avoid bizarre or distracting items* of *clothing, shoes, or jewelry.* You want the audience to concentrate on your message.

## Good Grooming Is a Must

It is not possible to give permanent prescriptions for hair-styles, either male or female. But the principle remains: Be a bit more conservative than the audience. A woman preacher should not have the most spectacular makeup in the room; a man preacher should not have the trendiest hair style.

Universally, however, the preacher should be scrupulously clean.

Beard? Okay, but don't look as if you just forgot to shave.

Long hair? Depends upon the circumstances, but it should not appear to have been untended for a month. Because of modern trends, in some congregations "modern looks" are acceptable, but cleanliness is *always* acceptable. So clean your fingernails, trim your beard, and always polish your shoes!

Also be particularly careful about keeping your breath fresh. If you have a chronic problem, get chlorophyll tablets from a health food store. People will want to talk to you and request personal prayer. So be sure your breath doesn't repel them. And don't chew gum to keep your breath fresh, because a gum-chewing, lip-smacking preacher offends many in the church.

## How to Use a Pulpit

From our modern point of view, the only practical use of a pulpit is to support a preacher's Bible and notes. It also represents

an obstacle that separates a speaker from his audience. But this was not always so. Traditionally, a pulpit sometimes stood as a symbol of divinely authorized pronouncements and Bible interpretation. In some churches, the pulpit is still reserved for ordained clergymen only. Other persons, such as worship leaders, address the congregation from a smaller pulpit or "lectern."

In some church traditions, the pulpit is never placed in the center of the platform. The thinking is that the pulpit is where a *man* stands, and *man* should never be central. An altar, representing the presence of God, is placed at the center. It is often a massive table, bearing candles and a cross.

In other traditions, the pulpit is always at the center because it is where the Word of God is preached, and the Word should always be central. Such churches usually have a different concept of the altar as well, seeing it as a place of repentance and dedication, not just a symbol of God's presence. In this case, the altar is a rail, a place for kneeling.

Until relatively recent times, a pulpit was not simply an upright piece of furniture — it was an elevated enclosure that had entry steps and a gate. This is why we still speak today of being "in" the pulpit.

Here's another interesting point: A "podium" is not a synonym for a pulpit. Although modern usage is changing its

meaning, a podium is actually something you stand upon, not something you stand behind.

Here is some good general information and some practical suggestions having to do with pulpits.

If possible, don't remain behind the pulpit permanently while you are preaching. You will usually have better rapport with your audience if you can get out from behind the barrier, at least part of the time.

Avoid using the pulpit for physical support. You won't project an image of strength if you appear to be held up by the pulpit. And pulpits are often flimsier than they look. Moldings and upper portions tend to be loose. Their slopes may be very steep, so be wary of the pulpit's reliability in holding your Bible and notes. If you don't pay attention, they both can slide over the flange onto the floor. And this is not a very "professional" look.

Finally, if you have a choice, use a small, less-conspicuous pulpit, rather than a large, massive one. The trend is toward less-obtrusive shapes, and many churches are using transparent models, which appear to remove the physical barrier between preacher and congregation. This is in line with our modern understanding that communication is better when there are fewer obstacles.

## Using a Microphone

As I have already expressed, I believe amplifiers are used in churches far more often than necessary. I still maintain that you

will develop a more natural and attractive speaking style if you can gain experience without the use of these artificial aids.

Nevertheless, public address systems are a fact of life for a preacher, and you will surely be using one. It is very unfortunate that so little orientation or instruction is available on the subject. What I offer here is not the professional word of a sound-systems expert, but I do believe my comments will help you generally in using a "mike."

Don't presume that the microphone will reliably do what you expect of it. The safest microphone to use is one you have already seen someone else use in the meeting. When you approach or pick it up, take notice to see if its switch is turned on. A clip-on wireless microphone's on/off switch is normally located on its belt-clipped FM transmitter. You will usually find the switch of a cordless hand mike in its base. And the on/off switch of a cord microphone is usually found near the top of the microphone shaft.

Don't test microphone volume by tapping or thumping it. This has been known to cause serious damage. It was designed to receive a voice, so test it by voice. If you are testing before a meeting while turning the system on, count to ten or recite the books of the Bible — anything but "thumping."

*Never* try to use a microphone while standing in front of a loudspeaker which is part of its amplifying system. That infamous squawk called audio "feedback" is caused by sound

coming out of the speaker and back into the microphone in an endless circuit.

When speaking into the microphone as you open a meeting, let your first sentence be something friendly and enthusiastic, but nothing so vital that your message will suffer if it isn't heard. The volume control in the sound booth may be inadvertently turned off or set at the wrong level, and the person at the console may need time to adjust it.

The most important DO for using a microphone is: *always keep it at a uniform distance from your mouth.* Whether you feel comfortable at three, six, or nine inches away, keep it there! Watch experienced professional speakers or singers live or on television. When you do, you will notice that no matter how much they move, lean, or gyrate, the microphone always stays fixed at the same point in front of the mouth. They have been coached in this manner by technicians and directors to ensure that their broadcast levels remain consistently the same. So go thou and do likewise.

Finally, don't form the habit (as many musicians do) of depending upon a loud monitor to direct your voice back to you. (It gives such a nice feeling of power!) You will develop a better sense of how well you are filling the room if you simply hear what comes back from the same loudspeakers the audience is hearing.

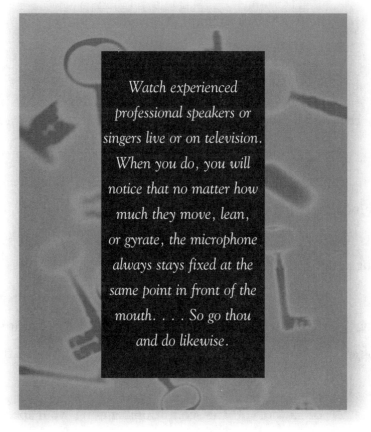

*Watch experienced professional speakers or singers live or on television. When you do, you will notice that no matter how much they move, lean, or gyrate, the microphone always stays fixed at the same point in front of the mouth. . . . So go thou and do likewise.*

When purchasing equipment for your church, don't presume that the latest gadget is always the best. Some of the new ultra-tiny lavaliere FM wireless microphones aren't as good in reproduction quality as the older larger models. And wireless microphones, though marvelously convenient, are several times more likely to give problems than conventional wired mikes.

Ask for the practical opinions of other public speakers before you buy.

## How to Get Sermon Ideas

In concluding this manual, I want to leave you with some of the ways I have discovered new sermon ideas over the years.

As a starting point of material development, never preach on a subject just because you happen to like it. Always keep in mind the people God has sent you to. Your sermons and lessons should always be related to their current needs. Here are some suggestions:

1. Read the Bible regularly, not just when you are preparing a sermon. In your devotional reading, the Holy Spirit will often call your attention to some passage containing a truth that your people need.

2. Be aware of the conditions among your people. Bereavement, celebration, special family events, commendable acts, even sins that come to your attention may be the beginning point for a sermon that will help the situation.

3. Keep up with current events that may be known to your people. Happenings in your country or the world, even tragic situations, may influence people in a way that will make them more receptive to certain truths at certain times.

4. Seek divine intervention. God may speak to you through circumstances or through the gifts of the Spirit, urging you to preach on a certain theme.

5. Develop a sense of balance. Don't just preach what comes easily. When you realize that some important doctrine hasn't been presented to your people for a long period of time, it is a good plan to build a sermon on that doctrine to ensure that your people have a good balance of truth.

6. Listen to the sermons of other preachers. You will occasionally hear another preacher's message that really grips and inspires you. But it probably won't work for you if you simply repeat it as you heard it. So improve upon it! Use the ideas, edited or supplemented, and empower them with your own illustrations. Or borrow the best illustrations for your own sermon. Use real names when possible and tasteful. Be not deceived, the best preachers borrow from each other continually. Give credit where credit is due, and develop the message afresh under God's anointing.

7. Utilize your own life experiences. Some of the strongest sermons come from the truths learned by personal experience. I have already recommended such experience as a source of illustrations, but a whole message can spring from some revelation made real to you by events from your own life. Jack Hayford and the late Jamie Buckingham, to name just two, are among the

highly respected preachers who have based their messages heavily upon their own experiences. Remember, a testimony of itself is not truly a sermon —but what happens to you in real life will often make a Scripture come alive in such a way that it gives you both text and structure for a sermon.

Finally, a preacher who is really in touch with God and with our needy world will find no lack of important subjects to preach about. Such subjects are everywhere around us. As long as God speaks to His world, His messengers will also speak.

Now, go and preach — not because you must say something, but because *you have something to say*.

# SAMPLES OF TEXTUAL OUTLINES

Psalm 1:1,4    TWO CLASSES OF PEOPLE
The blessed man (v.1)
The ungodly man (v.4)

Psalm 24:3,4    THE PERSON GOD BLESSES
Right actions (hands)
Right thoughts (heart)
Right worship (not idols)
Right words (not deceitfully)

APPENDIX

| Micah 6:8 | **WHAT GOD REQUIRES** |
| | Justice |
| | Mercy |
| | Humility |

| Matthew 2:11 | **RESPONSES TO JESUS** |
| | They saw |
| | They worshipped |
| | They gave |

| Matthew | **PUTTING THINGS IN ORDER** |
| | 5:24: Right relationships (first your brother; then your worship) |
| | 6:33: Right values (first the Kingdom, then other things) |
| | 7:5: Right correction (first the plank, then the speck) |

| Matthew 15:23,26,28 | **THREE ANSWERS TO PRAYER** |
| | Silence (not a word) |
| | Discouragement (it is not good) |
| | Miracle response (let it be on you) |

| Luke 9:11 | **JESUS' ATTITUDE TOWARD PEOPLE** |
| | Openness (He received them) |

Communication (He spoke to them)

Meeting needs (He healed them)

Luke 9:23      THE MEANING OF DISCIPLESHIP

Total renunciation (let him deny himself)

Daily renewal (take up your cross daily)

Close relationship (follow Me!)

Luke 18:36-43      STEPS TO A MIRACLE

He heard (v.36)

He cried out (v.39)

He prayed specifically (v.41)

He received (v.43)

John 14:      WHAT JESUS PROMISES

A place (v.2: "I go to prepare")

A power (vv.12-14: "Greater works than these")

A Presence (v.16: "Another helper… forever")

A peace (v.27: "My peace…not as the world gives")

Romans 1:8-16      QUALITIES OF A MINISTER

Gratitude (v.8: I thank)

Prayer (v.9: Always in prayers)

Fellowship (v.12: Encouraged together
with you)

Duty (v.14: I am debtor)

Boldness (v.16: I am not ashamed)

Romans 10:14,15    THE NECESSITY OF MISSIONS
How shall they call?
How shall they believe?
How shall they hear?
How shall they preach?

Romans 12:6-8    WAYS FOR BELIEVERS TO SERVE
Prophesying
Helping others
Teaching
Advising
Giving
Administering
Showing mercy

John Garlock (M.A. Christian Education) is the former direc-
tor of Christ For the Nations Institute, Dallas, Texas, where he
also taught missions, homiletics, cross-culture communication,
and other subjects. He has served as academic dean of
Continental Bible College, Brussels, Belgium; principal of
South African Bible Institute, Johannesburg; instructor of mis-
siology at Central Bible Institute and editor of missions publications for the Gospel Publishing House, both located in
Springfield, Missouri.

The son of pioneer Africa missionary H. B. Garlock
(author of *Before We Kill and Eat You*, an account of his work
among cannibal tribes), John is a distinguished "bush" pilot
who has preached the truth of Scripture in more than forty
countries around the world.

Other ministry training publications authored by Rev.
Garlock include *Teaching as Jesus Taught*, *Our World Witness*
(which he co-authored with Noel Perkin), and the Book of
Proverbs study notes contained in Thomas Nelson's *Spirit Filled
Life Bible*.

John resides near San Antonio in Bulverde, Texas, with his
wife Ruthanne, who travels and teaches with him extensively
in seminars in many countries.